GROWING AND LEARNING

The Playful Toddler

130+ Quick Brain-Boosting Activities for 18 to 36 Months

By
Becky Daniel

Illustrations by
Luanne Voltmer Marten

Publisher
Instructional Fair • T.S. Denison
Grand Rapids, Michigan 49544

About the Author

Becky Daniel is a parent, teacher, author, and editor—four distinctive yet interrelated professions. After graduating from California University at Long Beach, she taught kindergarten through eighth grade. When she began her family, she left the classroom to care for her first daughter and to pursue a career in writing at home.

Now the mother of three children—Amy, Sarah, and Eric—she edits a magazine and writes educational books from her home in Orcutt, California. Over the past 25 years she has written over 200 educational resource books.

She is also the author of a picture book, *Prince Poloka of Uli Loko,* a Hawaiian story for children, and *I Love You Baby,* a parenting book. In 1989 she was honored to have her biographical sketch and a list of her earlier works featured in Volume 56 of *Something About the Author.*

Credits

Author	Becky Daniel
Inside Illustrations	Luanne Voltmer Marten
Project Director	Debra Olson Pressnall
Editors	Debra Olson Pressnall & Karen Seberg
Cover Art Direction/Design	Terri Moll
Graphic Layout & Icon Illustrations	Mark Conrad
Cover Photograph	© EyeWire

ISBN:1-56822-954-2
Growing and Learning: The Playful Toddler
©2000 Instructional Fair • TS Denison
A Division of Instructional Fair Group, Inc.
A Tribune Education Company
3195 Wilson Drive NW, Grand Rapids, MI 49544

Dear Parents,

The coming year will be an exciting one for you and your toddler. It will also be a crucial time in your child's education. If you are a parent who feels that children should be intellectually enriched early on, you may be searching for resources and learning tools. If so, *Playful Toddler* was written especially for you! This book will help you understand the basic developmental stages for 18- to 36-month-old children and offer you simple games and activities to enrich your child's learning at each stage of development.

Fortunately, most toddlers are curious creatures. On their own, they will master fine- and gross-motor skills needed to do many things for themselves. However, if provided the appropriate toys and direction, a toddler will not only entertain himself for hours on end, he will master important skills. As a parent, you have the capability of giving your child exactly what he needs for intellectual stimulation.

In this book, you will find simple games and activities to help you build upon what your toddler can already do and enrich her intellectual growth. Do you know that scribbling with crayons or finger painting as well as dressing oneself and eating food are great eye-hand coordination activities? With a little direction, your toddler can turn everyday happenings into valuable learning experiences.

There is no best way to present the activities herein. How you use the learning activities will depend upon your unique child. The important thing to remember is your attitude while working with the toddler. Not only are the words you say important, but the way you say them communicates a message to your child. Be positive and complimentary when working with your toddler. No matter how many times it takes him to master something, verbally recognize the good in each attempt. You have the power to hold up a positive mirror to your toddler—one that will reflect how wonderful he is. Your kind words and encouragement will help your child feel worthwhile and capable of learning.

Sincerely,

Becky Daniel

TABLE OF CONTENTS

PLAYING WITH YOUR 24- TO 36-MONTH-OLD

I'll Do It Myself!
Fine Motor Development

Play, Baby, Play
Gross Motor Development

Let's Talk
Language Development

One, Two, Red, Blue
Cognitive/Creative Development

"Please" and "Thank You"
Social/Emotional Development

VALUE OF PLAY

Albert Einstein once said that the single most important decision any of us will ever make is whether or not to believe the universe is friendly. Play is the place where your toddler will begin to feel the joy of learning new things. Through her play interactions, your toddler will make a decision about life that will be a part of her very being for all of her days.

When your child was born he had over a hundred billion brain cells. Through play, trillions of synapses develop connecting these hundred billion cells in the brain. Each time your toddler is touched, hears a story, plays a game—every time he is interacted with, new synapses develop and the child's intellect is enhanced. Play, although it sounds simple, must be taken seriously. Play is your child's work!

Physically, a child develops well-balanced, fine and gross motor skills during recreation. Toys are not just objects of amusement. It is no accident that down through history, in all cultures, toys are a part of early childhood. Games with equipment teach the learner how to manipulate and like the old adage says, "Practice makes perfect." Mother Goose rhymes, musical games, and dancing about is play with rhythm and rhyme that orchestrates balance, coordination, and grace.

Emotionally, play is therapeutic. Since play is a natural medium for self-expression, it provides the child with a safe space to experience, express, and celebrate feelings. In play, the child is given the opportunity to "play" out his accumulated feelings of tension, frustration, insecurity, aggression, fear, bewilderment, confusion. The more difficult and less obvious advantage of play is that it allows a child a place to learn how to handle anger and aggression. Although this is a long process, expressing turmoil openly in socially acceptable ways is vital for a child's emotional well-being. As a bonus, through play, children develop a sense of humor and an ability to show empathy to others. Emotionally speaking, play is vital to mental health and stability. Playing in play groups gives children the opportunities to learn social skills: sharing, taking turns, and cooperation. Patterns of behavior, acceptable ways to interact, and ways of playing safely are also part of this whole socialization process.

Creativity is a tremendous gift with which human beings are born. Unfortunately, instead of being nurtured, often imaginations are stifled. As parents and caregivers of young children, we must remember: in fantasy play, children are given a stage on which they can spotlight their creative nature. Children imagine whole scenarios and assimilate their learning through fanciful make–believe. Symbolic play, in which toys and dolls are used, allows children an opportunity to practice every possible social situation. They can rehearse all the different roles and experience being whatever they choose. This exploratory play and experience with others is a prerequisite for the child to accomplish a positive self-image. And last but not least, it is through fantasy play that youngsters develop their sense of humor, practice empathy, and celebrate compassion.

Everyone senses on some level that the ability to be spontaneous and to play is a basic need and an important characteristic of healthy human beings. However, not everyone can channel this force for ultimate health and happiness. Unfortunately, learning to play is something we must do as children; if we do not learn how to play as a youngster, often it is a skill that cannot be learned as an adult. As parents and caregivers of young children, I urge you to teach your child how to use her brain, body, emotions, and imagination as vehicles for celebrating her higher self. When you teach your child to play, you are showing her the path of intellectual, social, and emotional transformation—a path which ultimately leads to self-actualization!

PLAYING

With Your Toddler

18- to 24-Months Old

I Can Do It!

Fine Motor Development

Contemplate

How does the old adage go? "Necessity is the mother of invention." Nothing could be more true for a toddler. Between 18 and 24 months, a toddler's fine motor skills increase in leaps and bounds because he needs to manipulate the world. Curiosity will keep a toddler engaged in small motor movements from sunrise to sunset. Nimble fingers poke and pinch; busy hands grasp and wave; limber arms carry and hug. During a toddler's second year, his fingers will master the coordination needed to hold a spoon, use a crayon, open a door, unwrap candy, pick up things, take things apart, and put things back together again. As time goes on, your toddler will become increasingly interested in more complex manipulations involving dials, switches, knobs, and locks. His construction skills will include: building towers and knocking them down, fitting things into other things, and emptying and refilling containers. Just as your toddler's fine motor development skyrockets, so will his pride in his accomplishments. One of his greatest joys will be the feeling that comes from knowing "I can do it!"

The new fine motor skills your toddler will acquire in the next six months are too numerous to list. Among his new skills will be variations of the following milestones.

Fine Motor Milestones: 18 to 24 Months

◆ Will learn how to scribble on paper when given a crayon
◆ Will learn how to manipulate finger paint
◆ Will learn how to turn over containers and pour out contents
◆ Will learn how to build towers of three to five blocks
◆ May begin showing a preference for his dominant hand
◆ Will learn how to fit round objects into round holes
◆ Will learn how to fit square objects inside square objects
◆ Will learn how to use modeling materials
◆ Will learn how to fit odd-shaped objects into containers
◆ Will learn how to clap hands
◆ Will learn how to drink from a cup and use a spoon
◆ Will learn how to put things into a paper bag and take them out again
◆ Will learn to put on and take off hats and caps

 General Tips

As a toddler becomes increasingly capable of exploring her environment through fine motor skills, she will need materials that support exploration and experimentation.

Appropriate toys for developing a toddler's fine motor skills include:

◆ Fat crayons and paper for scribbling
◆ Finger paints and finger painting paper
◆ Watercolors and watercolor brushes
◆ Poster paints, large brushes, and easel
◆ Puzzles with little knob handles
◆ Wooden blocks in varying sizes
◆ Sandbox with small shovels, buckets, cups, and spoons
◆ Water toys and tubs of water for play
◆ Containers that fit inside each other
◆ Cardboard boxes of all sizes for stacking and putting things into them

Craft projects using crayons, watercolor markers, play clay, paints, and paintbrushes will provide fine motor skill practice, too. Support your toddler in a variety of craft experiences. Doing crafts to provide these kinds of experiences for a toddler requires preparation and clean-up time and much effort. Although it will take planning and supervision on your part, the benefits for your youngster will be well worth the effort. It is through creative play that your child will learn to use her hands in skillful ways and gain positive self-esteem.

Mealtime is another excellent opportunity for your toddler to practice her fine motor skills. Always encourage your toddler to feed herself. Gripping small bits of food with fingers is good fine motor and eye-hand coordination practice. Removing raisins or small chunks of soft cheese from a plastic bowl will give your toddler an opportunity to practice the pincher grip. Holding a spoon and eating will give your toddler practice grasping with her fist.

Through touch, human beings "speak" very loudly. When touches are gentle, patient, and caring they send a clear message to the receiver. Hold hands with your child. Practice your own "fine motor skills" by gently patting and rubbing your child. Bonding with your toddler will be greatly enhanced by your loving hands.

Fine Motor Development 18- to 24-Month-Old

Scribble, Scribble

Purple, yellow, red, and blue,
Scribble, scribble, scribble do!

Overture

Holding a crayon in the writing position is a skill that your toddler will learn with practice. In the beginning, he will most likely grasp it in his fist and use it in an awkward way. Demonstrate how to hold the crayon in the proper position, but at first, do not expect him to have the fine motor skills required to hold a crayon correctly for writing. Let him scribble holding the crayon any way that is comfortable for him. In time, he will learn to hold the crayon between his thumb and index finger.

Performance

Play: To help your toddler learn how to manipulate crayons, play "Scribble, Scribble."
What you will need: Box of large crayons, large sheets of paper, newspaper
How to play: Cover a work surface with newspaper, then place a large sheet of paper on top of the newspaper. An appropriate work surface might be a desk or table where your toddler can work. If it is comfortable for him, the tray of his high chair can be used for a work surface. Open the box of crayons and show them to your toddler. Scribble on a sheet of paper where he can watch. Hand your toddler a crayon for scribbling. If need be, use your hand placed over his to guide him to move the crayon on the surface of the paper. Verbally encourage all efforts, even if the scribbling is off the paper. Do not define the child's drawing by suggesting it is anything except scribbles or demonstrate how to draw a familiar object. Simply scribble with the child. Say things like: "Your scribbling is beautiful." Or, "I like the way you scribble with the red crayon."

Finale

While scribbling with only four crayons, purple, yellow, red, and blue, sing the rhyme to the tune of "Twinkle, Twinkle, Little Star." When you sing the color of the crayon you are using, hold it up. For example, while coloring with a yellow crayon, every time you sing "yellow" hold it up. No need to talk about it; the point is just that colors have names, not which color has which name. On other occasions, make up new rhymes and substitute other colors in the rhyme; scribble with those colors. Example:

> Orange, black, green, and tan,
> Scribble, scribble, if you can.

Encore

Let your toddler know that his artwork is treasured by celebrating it.
- ◆ Frame his scribbling and hang it in your home.
- ◆ Have him scribble in a notebook, and keep it in a safe place to show him when he is older.
- ◆ Send his pages of scribbling to relatives.
- ◆ Use scribbled newsprint to wrap presents.

Swirl the Colors

Roses are red; violets are blue,
I like to finger paint, and so do you.

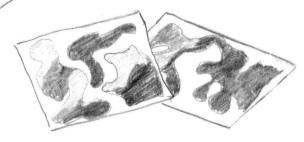

Overture

Watch to see how your toddler begins to use her hands in coordination with eye movements. Finger painting offers the unique experience of seeing how fingers can move.

Performance

Play: Give your toddler an opportunity to finger paint; play "Swirl the Colors."
What you will need: Red and blue finger paints, finger paint paper, newspaper
How to play: Cover the work surface with newspaper. Place a large sheet of wet finger-paint paper on the newspaper. Place several spoonfuls of red finger paint on the wet paper. Demonstrate how to use fingers to move the paint on the paper. Let your toddler use the finger paints to swirl colorful red designs. After awhile, add a dab of blue finger paint and swirl it into the red.

Finale

Recite the rhymes while swirling finger paint with fingers. Create original rhymes when using combinations of the other primary colors: yellow and red, or blue and yellow. Example:

> Ducks are yellow; trucks are red.
> Let's finger paint 'til it's time for bed!

Encore

On other occasions, use new versions of the rhyme to describe special things about your toddler.
Examples:

> Roses are red; violets are blue,
> Peaches are soft, and so are you.

> Sunsets are red; the sky is blue,
> Clouds are beautiful, and so are you.

> Fire engines are red; the ocean is blue,
> Trees grow strong, and so do you.

Rusty, Dusty, Dump Truck

Oh, the little rusty, dusty, dump truck!
Moves along the rusty, dusty, dirt road.

Overture

Fascination with cars and trucks begins at a very early age. Large plastic vehicles that can be pushed or pulled hold special interest for toddlers. Tiny cars that can be moved on dirt or in sand will acquaint your child with words like "up," "down," "in," "out," "over," "through," and "under."

Performance

Play: To encourage your toddler to put things into empty containers, play "Rusty, Dusty, Dump Truck."

What you will need: Large, plastic dump truck (or a large shoe box with one end removed), wooden blocks

How to play: Put a pile of blocks in one area of the room. Place several blocks in the bed of the dump truck (or shoe box). Scoot it along the floor or ground like a dump truck carrying a heavy load along a dusty, dirt road. Then lift one end of the truck's bed (or shoe box) so the blocks slide out the open end in dump-truck fashion. Scoot the dump truck back over to the pile of blocks and load it up again. After demonstrating, let your toddler use the truck to transport blocks. Soon he will be playing with the blocks and truck, and dumping loads of blocks on his own.

Finale

Recite the rhyme while pushing toy cars or trucks along paths in sand or on the sidewalk. Use dump trucks to transport wooden blocks from one area to another. Recite the rhyme while your toddler plays with the blocks and truck. While driving in the car, when you see a large dump truck loaded down with its cargo, recite the rhyme. Create elevated planes made of cardboard and use them in various ways:

- ◆ Slide blocks down a ramp.
- ◆ Race two cars at a time down a ramp.
- ◆ Roll small rubber balls down a ramp.
- ◆ Push toy cars up a ramp.

Encore

When playing with tiny toy cars, often the most exciting terrain for driving the toy cars is another person's body. Try pushing a tiny car over your toddler's legs and feet. Stop at the knee and say something like this: "This is Knee Mountain." Then push on to the ankle, foot, and toes. "Here we are at Toe City." Race around your toddler's belly or up and down his back. Of course, let your toddler have the chance to gently push the car around on your arms and legs, too.

Tip, Top, Tower

Tip, top, tower,
Tumble down in an hour.

Overture

Long before toddlers show an interest in building block towers, they relish knocking them down. Observe your toddler at play, and you will see how pleased she is when her actions cause reactions. Knocking down a tower of blocks is very exciting for most children this age. Toddlers attain a sense of power when they know they are responsible for the loud crashes that follow the tipping of a block tower.

Performance

Play: To encourage your toddler to build towers of three to five blocks, play "Tip, Top, Tower."
What you will need: Wooden blocks
How to play: Sit on the floor with a pile of blocks between you and your toddler. Begin by stacking one block on top of another. Then gently knock off the top block. Next, build a tower of three blocks. Again knock off the top blocks. Try building a tower of four blocks. In the beginning, do not build towers larger than five or six blocks. Set up block towers for your toddler to knock down. Help your toddler build small towers and knock them down together.

Finale

Use the rhyme shown above when building and knocking down blocks. Recite the rhyme; on the word "tumble" knock down the blocks. On other occasions, build tall block towers. Recite the rhyme, and on the word "tumble" encourage your toddler to knock down the tower. Youngsters really enjoy causing block towers to tumble to the ground. Build towers with four blocks as the foundation so they are more difficult to knock down. Playing with blocks is even more fun when toy cars and trucks are incorporated into the play. Use the blocks to build bridges, roads, and parking garages.

Encore

Use shoe boxes and other small boxes with tight-fitting lids for building towers. Demonstrate for your toddler how the bigger boxes go on the bottom, pyramid-style. Even larger boxes with lids can be used to build towers. Toddlers enjoy building and knocking down towers—the bigger the better! Other materials besides wooden blocks and cardboard boxes suitable for building towers are egg cartons, plastic bowls and cups, and plastic food tubs with lids.

Animal Crackers

Take a cup, and drink it up,
And call your neighbors in.

Overture

Watch to see if your toddler demonstrates a clear tendency toward right or left-handedness. Some children do not show a preference for several years. Other young children are ambidextrous and can use both hands equally well. There is no reason to pressure your toddler to use one hand more than the other or to rush the natural process. Just observe it.

Performance

Play: To see if your child has a tendency to use a dominant hand, have a tea party with animal crackers.

What you will need: Plastic toy dishes (cups, saucers, plates), basket of animal crackers, bite-sized crackers or graham crackers

How to play: Use a baby blanket on the floor to indicate the tea party spot. Set the plastic toy dishes, cups, and saucers on the blanket. Place a basket of animal crackers in the center of the blanket. Seat your toddler in front of a place setting. Some toddlers will be eager to have a pretend tea party, while others cannot yet participate at a cooperative level. Pretend to pour tea. Invite your toddler to have an animal-shaped cookie by holding the basket out to him. Watch to see which hand he uses to take the treat. Repeat several times. Also watch to see which hand he uses to hold the cup when pretending to drink tea. If your toddler is not ready to sit on a blanket for a quiet time but would rather play randomly with dishes, pick up these cues and follow his lead. Your tea party should be just that—a "party" and enjoyed any way it unfolds.

Finale

Use the above rhyme during the tea party. When you say "drink it up," pause to take a pretend drink from your cup. On other occasions, when encouraging your child to finish a glass of milk, recite the rhyme, "Take a cup and drink it up." Any time your toddler is having a snack can become time for a tea party. Bite-sized pieces of soft cheese and goldfish-shaped crackers make good tea party foods. Put milk, water, or juice in the teapot and pour a party for two. Ordinary occasions can be boring, but with a little imagination, anything done with your toddler can become a celebration! Your toddler will enjoy doing things twice as much if he is sharing it with you.

Encore

Picnics and parties offer a perfect setting for your toddler to practice filling and emptying containers. Small pieces of food like doughnut-shaped cereal or raisins are especially good for games that involve transferring. Place two or more containers on a table, then put the food in one of them. Show your toddler how to redistribute the food among the containers. For non-food play, water and sand are both very good for filling and emptying containers, too.

Will It Fit?

Eggs in a carton,
One. Two. Three.

Overture

Watch how your toddler examines the things that she picks up. Now that she can manipulate small objects at will, she will explore all the ways she can hold and use objects.

Performance

Play: To help your toddler learn how to put round objects into round holes, play "Will It Fit?"

What you will need: Styrofoam egg carton, six plastic eggs (that will fit in the carton), six wooden blocks

How to play: Place the six plastic eggs in the carton. Let your toddler observe how they rest neatly in the sections. Then have your toddler observe as you try to fit the square wooden blocks into the carton. Empty the carton. One at a time, hold up an egg or block and ask, "Will it fit?" Try each one. Continue asking each time you try an object and verbally respond with "Yes, it fits," or "No, it won't fit." Then let the toddler have free play with the carton, eggs, and blocks.

Finale

Recite the above rhyme while your toddler plays with the carton and plastic eggs. On other occasions, use the rhyme when cracking eggs at breakfast or for baking. When you buy eggs at the store, recite the rhyme to your toddler. Make sure she has egg cartons for play. Include Styrofoam cartons. Styrofoam egg cartons with the tops cut off make great bins for plastic eggs. Some toddlers this age enjoy putting eggs in the sections and taking them out again.

Encore

Provide a wide variety of shapes of containers for holding the smaller objects:
- ◆ Cupcake pan
- ◆ Plastic milk jug with a handle and no lid
- ◆ Small cookie, gourmet coffee, or tea tins without lids
- ◆ Cardboard oatmeal box
- ◆ Plastic cup with handle
- ◆ Plastic pitcher with handle
- ◆ Plastic bucket with handle

Also provide a variety of shapes of objects for filling the containers:
- ◆ Wooden blocks in different shapes
- ◆ Plastic straws
- ◆ Empty spice containers
- ◆ Plastic eggs
- ◆ Sponges cut in interesting shapes
- ◆ Large wooden beads

Box It Up

Round about, round about, Sweetie-pie.
You loves boxes, and so do I.

Overture

Toddlers learn a great deal through experimentation. Watch and you will see your toddler's delight when he discovers how something works. Young children develop patience, determination, and perseverance when fitting boxes inside each other.

Performance

Play: To help your toddler learn how to fit round objects inside round objects and square objects inside square objects, play "Box It Up."

What you will need: Four boxes including: large, round, ice cream carton with lid; smaller round box such as oatmeal carton (cut so it will fit inside the round ice cream pail); square box with lid; smaller square box that will fit inside the square box

How to play: Place all four boxes on the table. Demonstrate how the smaller round box will fit inside the ice cream carton and how the smaller square box will fit inside the larger square box. Then let your toddler use the boxes for experimentation.

Finale

Recite the rhyme while working with the boxes. Add other boxes that may or may not fit inside the large round and large square boxes. Try putting blocks in the square boxes and plastic eggs in the round boxes. On other occasions, use the rhyme while playing with large boxes. Place a huge sturdy box on the floor where your toddler can crawl inside and sit and play.

Encore

So your toddler will discover how things fit together, provide a variety of objects for nesting and stacking. Look around the house and you will find many containers that your toddler can use to fill and empty. Include some of these:

◆ Large plastic bowls that nest within each other make good play things. Demonstrate how to nest the bowls and how to turn them over and stack them to build towers.

◆ Soft, cloth suitcases also make great containers for filling.

◆ A basket large enough to hold a beach ball will offer your toddler many moments of fun putting the ball inside the basket and then trying to get it out again. Watch to see if your toddler learns to tip the basket so the ball will roll out.

◆ Plastic trash cans are also good for holding blocks or stuffed animals.

Clay Play

Pat-a-cake, pat-a-cake, baker's man!
Make me a cake as fast as you can.
Pat it, and prick it, and mark it with "B,"
And there will be enough for Baby and me.
—Traditional Rhyme

Overture

Watch and you will notice that your toddler moves constantly. Providing highly motivating activities that will focus her attention for short spurts will give her time to relax and help extend her attention span. Watch your toddler when she is engaged in something she finds fascinating, and you will see that she truly can focus for extended periods of time.

Performance

Play: To help your toddler learn how to use modeling material, arrange for many opportunities to play with clay. Clay is great for fine motor practice.

What you will need: Store-bought dough for playing—the more colorful the better, flat surface such as a cutting board

How to play: Demonstrate how to roll balls in the palms of your hands. You will need to do this for your toddler. Then show her how to roll the dough on a flat surface. To make a "cake," flatten a ball of clay with the palm of the hand. Give the toddler dough and help her roll it into a ball and flatten it with the palm of her hand. Any shape your toddler wants to make with the clay is okay. Just being able to mold it and change its shape will be a pleasant experience for your youngster.

Finale

Recite the nursery rhyme while making clay "cakes." On other occasions, use the rhyme in the kitchen while you are baking or preparing food for snack time. Use the rhyme to clap and keep time to a beat.
Example:
Pat-a-cake (*clap*), pat-a-cake (*clap*), baker's (*clap*) man (*clap*)!
Make me (*clap*) a cake (*clap*) as fast (*clap*) as you can (*clap*).
Pat it (*clap*), and prick it (*clap*), and mark it (*clap*) with "B" (*clap*),
And there (*clap*) will be (*clap*) enough for (*clap*) Baby and me (*clap*).

Encore

Modeling things besides clay is also fun for toddlers. When you bake bread, give your toddler a small handful of dough to knead. If you do not bake bread, buy frozen loaves of bread dough. Thaw one and let your toddler help you knead the bread. Then put the dough in a buttered pan, cover with a clean cloth, and place it in a warm place until it rises. Look at the bread dough. Let the toddler see how big the dough rises. Punch it down, and knead it again. Again, let the dough rise. Bake it and serve warm slices with butter. Your toddler will enjoy seeing the bread dough rise, touching the dough, smelling it as it bakes, and then tasting the delicious flavor of homemade bread. On another occasion, form the dough into balls, sprinkle them with cinnamon and sugar, and bake the cinnamon buns.

Pick Up Sticks

> . . . *Five, six, pick up sticks;*
> *Seven, eight, lay them straight. . . .*
> —Traditional Rhyme

Overture..

Watch your toddler playing, and you will see an enormous amount of energy coupled with a very short attention span. When playing learning games with your toddler, keep the sessions as short as possible. A game that takes three to ten minutes may be all your toddler can handle. When your toddler shows disinterest, end the session or let him play with the toys.

Performance..

Play: To encourage your toddler to fit odd-shaped objects into a container, play "Pick Up Sticks."
What you will need: Colorful plastic drinking straws; large, round, plastic ice cream carton
How to play: Place the straws on the floor. Demonstrate how to pick up straws one at a time and put them in the bucket. Then dump the straws out again. Let your toddler experiment with fitting the straws into the bucket. (Flexible straws are good for this game because they will give and fit into the bucket without going in straight.)

Finale...

Use the first line of the above rhyme while putting straws into the bucket. Use the second line while taking them out and "laying them straight." On other occasions, give the straws to the toddler for play. Replace the large ice cream bucket with a tall plastic glass. See if your toddler can place some straws into a smaller container. As an assisted learning experience, construct play clay and drinking straw creations. Roll small balls of play clay. Stick the ends of the straws into the clay to make a creative three-dimensional structure. The play clay works well for the joints between the straws.

Encore..

Here is a recipe you can make if your toddler likes to eat the dough as well as play with it:

Peanut Butter Play Dough
½ cup (118 ml) of peanut butter
3½ tablespoons (53 ml) powdered milk
½ tablespoon (8 ml) honey or corn syrup
Directions: Mix all the ingredients together in a bowl until smooth. Add more powdered milk if the dough is too sticky. Add a little more honey if the dough is too dry. Cover the play surface with waxed paper and refrigerate any leftover dough. After your toddler finishes her creation, decorate it with raisins, cut dried fruit, etc. Then enjoy eating it!

Clap, Clap Hands

Clap, clap hands, Mommy's wee, wee one;
Clap, clap hands, Daddy's coming home. . . .
—Traditional Rhyme

Overture

Watch your toddler learning to clap, and you will see that clapping her hands together takes a great deal of coordination. To begin teaching your toddler to clap, rest the heels of both hands together. Then bring her fingers together and apart, together and apart. Keeping the heels of her hands touching will make clapping much easier.

Performance

Play: To help your toddler learn how to clap hands to a beat, play "Clap, Clap Hands."
What you will need: No special equipment is needed to play this game.
How to play: Introduce the rhyme two lines at a time. Hold the toddler in your lap. Hold her hands in your hands. Clap on each beat of the rhyme as follows:

Clap (*clap*), clap (*clap*) hands (*clap*),
Mommy's (*clap*) wee (*clap*), wee (*clap*) one (*clap*);
Clap (*clap*), clap (*clap*) hands (*clap*),
Daddy's (*clap*) coming (*clap*) home (*clap*).
Home to (*clap*) his bonny (*clap*) wee one (*clap*);
Clap (*clap*), clap (*clap*) hands (*clap*),
My wee (*clap*), wee (*clap*) one (*clap*).

Finale

When your toddler learns to clap in rhythm, recite the rhyme and let her clap on her own.

Encore

On other occasions, recite the first four lines of the verse, and use a variety of actions. Use feet to keep the beat of the rhyme. Move around in a circle. Have the toddler join in each action you name and demonstrate.

Stomp (*stomp*), stomp (*stomp*) feet (*stomp*),
Mommy's (*stomp*) wee (*stomp*), wee (*stomp*) one (*stomp*);
Stomp (*stomp*), stomp (*stomp*) feet (*stomp*),
Daddy's (*stomp*) coming (*stomp*) home (*stomp*).

Try these movements, too:
◆ March (*Lift knees high.*)
◆ Tiptoe

     **19**

Bread and Jam Picnic

A glass of milk and a slice of bread,
And then good night, we must go to bed.
—Traditional Rhyme

Overture

Toddlers of eighteen months can learn to use spoons to eat, but on some days, they may want to regress to fingers. Providing foods that can be eaten with a spoon or fingers is the best way to handle self-feeding. Let your toddler choose and progress from finger feeding to using a spoon at his own unique rate.

Performance

Play: To give your toddler practice drinking from a plastic cup with a handle and using plastic eating utensils, have a "Bread and Jam Picnic."
What you will need: Plastic cup, milk, bread and jam, plastic spoons
How to play: If weather permits, have the bread and jam picnic outside on a warm day. Place a baby blanket on the grass or floor to indicate the picnic spot. Sit on the blanket. Allow the toddler to help spread jam on his bread with a spoon. This is a good opportunity for your toddler to drink from a cup without worrying about spilling.

Finale

Use the nursery rhyme while preparing the picnic sandwiches. Use another version of the verse while eating other meals.
Example:
  Scrambled eggs and a slice of toast,
  Which do you like the most?

Encore

On other occasions when buying bread or milk, putting away groceries, pouring milk for dinner, or making toast in the morning, recite the rhyme. When you say "bread," hold up a loaf or slice of bread. When you say "milk," hold up the milk. When serving a snack, recite a new version of the rhyme replacing the foods mentioned with the appropriate ones.
Examples:
  A slice of apple and a cup of water,
  Enjoy them both, my darling daughter.

  A cup of milk and one warm bun,
  Enjoy them both, my loving son.

  A crispy cracker and a chunk of cheese,
  Eat them both, if you please.

Bag It!

Big bags, little bags.
Big, brown grocery bags.

Overture

There is a time when toddlers begin to enjoy imitating what they see others do. Sometimes more complicated games can be played by your toddler if you demonstrate the task ahead of time.

Performance

Play: To help your toddler learn how to put things into a bag and take them out again, play "Bag It!"
What you will need: Large, brown grocery bag; toys that will fit inside the bag
How to play: Roll the top edge of the paper bag down several times to make a sturdy container that will stand upright on the floor. Select toys that will fit inside the bag and set them on the floor next to the bag. Show the toddler how to place one toy in the bag, then take it out. Repeat with another toy. The bag should be large enough that individual toys can be easily slipped inside it and removed or poured out. Place a toy inside the bag and ask, "Where is the toy?" Let your toddler remove the toy from the bag. Then give instructions such as, "Put the bear inside the bag." Repeat naming each toy. If the toddler has difficulty putting specific toys in the bag, just let her practice putting things into the bag and then taking them out again.

Finale

Use another version of the rhyme and two different sized bags—large grocery bag and a small lunch bag (with sides rolled down to make them sturdy) and a variety of toys that will fit inside the bags. Put a toy inside one of the bags as you recite a new version of the rhyme.
Example:
    Big bag, little bag.
    Bear is inside the big bag.
Name the toy that is inside the bag. Give the toddler the bag and let her remove the toy. Encourage your toddler to put a toy in a bag. Recite the rhyme with each new toy, then remove it. Experiment with a variety of sizes of bags and toys to find out which toys will fit in which bags. Use a version of this game in different rooms of your home and vary the objects inside the bags. Play games with a theme of kitchen tools, clothing, foods, etc. Name the object placed in the bag by reciting the new rhyme. Then, recite the rhyme with the name of an object, and let your toddler place the appropriate item in the bag and take it out.

Encore

Middle-sized bags (smaller than grocery bags and larger than lunch sacks) can be used to make good, sturdy derby-shaped hats. Scrunch a bag and then lay it out flat. Roll the top edge of the bag down again and again until it looks like a derby. Scrunch the whole hat, and then smooth it out again. Create a sturdy derby that your toddler can wear. The derby can be decorated with crayons, markers, stickers, feathers, dried flowers, etc. Your toddler might enjoy helping you make or decorate the derby.

Put It On, Take It Off

Come take up your hats, and away let us haste,
To the butterfly's ball, and the grasshopper's feast. . . .
—Traditional Rhyme

Overture..

Watch your toddler, and you may notice that he is beginning to put things where they belong. Children this age have a concept of orderliness. Given a hat, a toddler will often put it on his head. He will try to pull socks onto his feet and put his arms in the sleeves of a coat.

Performance...

Play: To encourage your toddler to put on and take off hats, play "Put It On, Take It Off."
What you will need: A variety of hats and caps that fit you and your toddler
How to play: Place a hat on your head. Take it off and give it to your toddler. Help him put it on his head. Then put on a different hat or cap. Repeat several times. Reverse roles. See if your toddler will offer you a hat or cap. After you finish playing with the hats and caps, make them available for the toddler's free play.

Finale..

To make playing with hats and caps even more fun, have your toddler sit in front of a full-length mirror with the hats and caps nearby. Allow time for the child to play with the hats and gaze into the mirror. Talk about the hats/caps:
   ◆ "This one is soft."
   ◆ "Look at you! You are wearing Grandpa's gardening hat."
   ◆ "I like the way you look in Grandma's straw hat."
   ◆ "This one is blue and red!"

Even though your toddler cannot answer you, ask him about the hats.
   ◆ "Which one do you like best?"
   ◆ "Do you know whose hat this is?"
   ◆ "Do you like the way you look in Daddy's baseball cap?"
   ◆ "This one is too small for me. Does it fit you?"

Use the rhyme when you are getting your toddler dressed in the morning, bundling him up for an outing, or at night when putting on his pajamas.

Encore..

Your toddler is probably beginning to learn how to dress himself. You can encourage your toddler to practice dressing skills as they spontaneously arise. Begin by having the toddler put on his hat, put one arm in the sleeve of a coat, or push his foot into a shoe while you are helping him get dressed. Getting dressed, like eating, can be played out with dolls and stuffed animals. Although your toddler will not have the fine motor skills needed to dress a doll, he may be able to undress it.

Keeping Track

Milestone	Date	Comments
Can scribble with a crayon		
Can swirl finger paint on paper		
Can turn over a container and pour out the contents		
Can build a three- to five-block tower/knock it down		
Shows a preference for left/right hand		
Can put round objects into round holes		
Can put square objects into square containers		
Can put round objects into round containers		
Can mold clay to form a shape		
Can put odd-shaped objects into a container		
Can clap (need not keep time)		
Can drink from a cup and use a spoon		
Can put objects into a bag and take them out again		
Can put on and take off a hat/cap		

On the Move

Gross Motor Development

Contemplate

Most toddlers love to dance, jog, twirl, and spin—celebrating all of their new motor skills. With a toddler's natural desire to move and explore, his newly acquired mobility and maturing gross motor skills make age-appropriate play and materials increasingly important. Although up until this time your toddler may have enjoyed playing in a small, confined area, no longer will a limited space be satisfactory. Children this age need to get out of the house, onto playgrounds and into play groups where their high-level energy can be expended. If not given the opportunity to put their energy into action in appropriate settings like a playground or fenced backyard, toddlers tend to act out in inappropriate ways. Make sure your toddler has plenty of room to practice gross motor development, promote body awareness, and stimulate creativity through his movement.

Although a toddler needs outdoor fun, an eighteen-month-old does not understand heights or the consequences of falling. Monitoring his play will become even more critical. A child this age cannot play outside—even in a fenced yard—unless he is constantly supervised. In the months ahead, a great deal of your time will be spent just watching your toddler play. The following are just a few games that will entertain and enhance gross motor skills for your toddler in the second half of his second year.

Gross Motor Milestones: 18 to 24 Months

◆ Will learn to walk (rarely falling anymore)
◆ Will learn to pull toys behind him
◆ Will begin to learn how to run (may not be smoothly)
◆ Will become aware of his own fingers, toes, hands, feet, arms, and legs
◆ Will learn how to stand on tiptoe (but not hold position)
◆ Will begin learning how to kick a large, stationary ball
◆ Will learn how to climb onto and down from furniture
◆ Will learn to sit down in and get up from a child-sized chair
◆ Will learn how to hop with feet together
◆ Will begin learning how to carry objects while walking
◆ Will learn how to stoop and pick up objects without falling over
◆ Will learn to move quickly by rolling over and over again
◆ Will begin to learn how to turn somersaults

 General Tips

The posture of children this age is often of concern to adults. Rest assured, a toddler's normal posture is sometimes a bit potbellied and swaybacked. It may look uncomfortable, but it is just a way of balancing the body in an upright position. As your toddler learns to walk and gains large motor skills, she will straighten up and stand tall.

During the second half of the second year, toddlers spend much of the day experimenting. They may try to climb into, upon, around, and under everything they see. They begin to enjoy simple games played with balls and playground equipment like swings and slides.

Toddlers love to wrestle and play. Physical contact that encourages gross motor skills, such as holding your toddler's hands and helping her leap or hop about will be fun and engaging for both of you. Teach her how to use the large muscles in her arms for big bear hugs and other ways of showing physical affection.

Provide appropriate equipment and toys for toddlers including:
- Simple, small doll carriage
- Wagon with a broad base (a low center of gravity to avoid tipping)
- Push and pull toys with rigid rods and blunt handles for easy grasping
- Soft, small lightweight ball
- Large rubber ball
- Beach ball
- Small, plastic, low slide (two or three steps)
- Child-sized rocking chair
- Large cardboard boxes for climbing into and around
- Laundry baskets for sorting/storing toys

Follow the Leader

Follow the leader, do as I do,
March. Stomp. Stop. Touch your shoe.

Overture

Watch your toddler, and you will catch him imitating the grown-ups around him. Often a boy this age will walk like his father; a girl will move like her mother. Toddlers copy the gestures they see happening around them. Your toddler's willingness to imitate can be a useful tool when teaching him important skills.

Performance

Play: To encourage your toddler's balanced walking, play "Follow the Leader."
What you will need: No special equipment is needed for this game.
How to play: Introduce the concept of following a leader by doing what the toddler is doing. Say something like this: "I am following your lead. I am doing what you do. You are the leader." When you think your child understands the concept, ask him to follow your lead. Invite him to "Follow the leader." Begin slowly. Just walk around in a circle. Then walk and pause, walk and pause. Slowly add variations of marching and stopping to the game. Include stopping to sit for a moment, stomping, running, waving your arms, etc. Allow your toddler an opportunity to be the leader and follow his movements.

Finale

Use the rhyme while following the leader. Make the appropriate movements as you slowly recite the rhyme, "March. Stomp. Stop. Touch your shoe." Change the words to the rhyme to include new instructions. Some examples include:
> Stop. Walk. Stop.
> Hop. Hop. Hop.
>
> Stoop. Droop. Drop.
> Stoop. Droop. Drop.
>
> March. Stop. March.
> Stop. March. Stop.

On other occasions, play a sitting down version of "Follow the Leader." Include: fine motor movements, clapping hands/slapping thighs, winking/blinking, touching face and body parts, wiggling fingers/toes, shaking/nodding head, lying down/sitting up, etc.

Encore

As your toddler develops the strength and coordination for a new level of vigor, he will also begin to enjoy imaginative play. Moving like animals makes for a very interesting "Follow the Leader" game. As you lead the game, you can demonstrate some different animal movements. Include:
- ◆ Hop like a frog. (*Squat and hop.*)
- ◆ Gallop like a horse. (*Lead with same foot.*)
- ◆ Crawl like a snake. (*Crawl flat on floor.*)
- ◆ Walk like a penguin. (*Heels together, toes out.*)

Moving the Toys

As I was going up and down, I met a little dandy,
Who pulled a wooden wagon, full of toys and candy.

Overture

Toddlers like to please the adults around them. Watch and you will see how your toddler looks to you for approval. Be aware of the look your toddler gives you when she wants your praise. Acknowledge her accomplishments often.

Performance

Play: To encourage your toddler to pull toys, play "Moving the Toys."

What you will need: A small sturdy wagon, toys that will fit inside the wagon

How to play: The object of the game is to move toys from one end of a room to the other. Demonstrate by placing a toy in the wagon and pulling it to the other end of the room. Take the toy out of the wagon and put it on the floor. Pull the wagon back to the pile of toys. Repeat these steps several times. Explain that you want to move the pile of toys from one place to the other. Ask the toddler to help you with the project. Then encourage your toddler to work on the project on her own. Praise the way she moves the toys. When everything has been moved, and if she is enjoying the game, use the wagon to move the toys back to the other side of the room or to another room.

Finale

Recite the rhyme as your toddler moves the toys. If working with your toddler inside the house, use a wagon to transport objects, such as folded socks from the laundry room to the appropriate bedroom, folded towels to appropriate bathroom, dish towels to the kitchen, etc. Inviting your toddler to help perform household chores will give her a great feeling of satisfaction.

Encore

On other occasions, when working in the yard, have the toddler use her wagon to move leaves to a barrel, weeds to a pile, garden vegetables to the porch, cut flowers to the patio, etc. When a child this age understands the "work" she is to do, she will spend a great deal of time and energy completing a task. Demonstrating how work can be made easier by using proper tools (such as a wagon for transporting objects) is a good lesson for a child this age.

Running Races

Run, run, run, as fast as you can.
You can't catch me, I'm the Gingerbread Man.
—"The Gingerbread Man"

Overture

Watch your child and you will notice that as your toddler becomes more steady on his feet, instead of walking, he may run from place to place.

Performance

Play: To practice running, play racing games.
What you will need: No special equipment is needed for this game.
How to play: Challenge your toddler to race you to a tree, fence, or other designated spot. Say something like this, "I'll race you to that tree." Then race back to the original spot. Try a variety of races including:

- *Around* a tree
- *Over* a hill
- *Under* a table
- *Between* two poles

Finale

Use the above rhyme and others to begin races. Other rhymes to begin races include:

Get ready.
Get set.
Go!

On your mark.
Get set.
Go!

You can also use racing as a way to get your child to do things that he does not want to do.
Examples:
"I'll race you to your bed."
"Can you climb into bed and cover up before I count to five?"
"Can you finish eating your cereal before I finish loading the dishes into the dishwasher?"

Encore

On other occasions, let your toddler "race" alone. Tell him, "Race over to that tree." Watch as he dashes from place to place. Tell your toddler how proud you are that he can run. Toddlers enjoy having an audience. Watching him run around will be all the motivation he needs to move at a quick pace and practice large motor skills. Remember, the more active he is during the day, the better he will sleep at night.

This Little Piggy

This little pig went to market.
This little pig stayed home.
This little pig had roast beef.
This little pig had none.
And this little piggy cried,
"Wee, wee," all the way home.
—Traditional Rhyme

Overture

Observe your toddler moving about, and you will see how fascinated she is with her own body—especially her fingers and toes. Toddlers sometimes become engrossed with their own hands and fingers. Walking barefoot, a toddler will often stop to look down at her own toes.

Performance

Play: To play a fingers and toes game, use the nursery rhyme "This Little Piggy."
What you will need: No special equipment is needed to play this game.
How to play: Place the toddler on the floor on her back. Remove her shoes and socks. Recite the nursery rhyme as you play with her toes. Use the rhyme to play with fingers, too.

This little pig went to market. (*Wiggle big toe.*)
This little pig stayed home. (*Wiggle second toe.*)
This little pig had roast beef. (*Wiggle middle toe.*)
This little pig had none. (*Wiggle fourth toe.*)
And this little piggy cried, (*Wiggle little toe.*)
"Wee, wee," all the way home.

Finale

Use other versions of the rhyme to celebrate other body parts. While your toddler is lying on the floor on her back, recite new versions and move appropriate body parts.
Examples:

This little leg walked to market. (*Hold toddler's foot; move leg.*)
This little leg went, too. (*Hold toddler's other foot; move leg.*)
This little hand bought apples. (*Pick up one hand.*)
This little hand carried them home. (*Pick up the other hand.*)
This little mouth ate the apples, (*Touch the toddler's lips.*)
Yum, yum, all the way home.

This little mouth sings a song. (*Touch lips.*)
These little ears hear the song. (*Touch ears.*)
These little legs dance and prance. (*Touch legs.*)
These little feet do a jig all the way home. (*Move feet as if dancing.*)

Encore

On other occasions, ask your toddler to demonstrate that she knows other body parts. Say, "Point to your arm" or "Point to your knees," etc.

Kick and Run

One for the money,
Two for the show,
Three to make ready,
Four to go!
—Traditional Rhyme

Overture

Watch your toddler at play, and you will see that he is becoming more coordinated each day. With practice he will learn how to lift one foot off the ground and still keep his balance.

Performance

Play: To practice kicking a large stationary ball, play "Kick and Run."
What you will need: Large rubber ball
How to play: This game should be played outside. Place the ball on the ground and demonstrate how to kick it. Then run and retrieve the ball. Place it in the original spot, kick it again, and retrieve it. When your toddler understands the object of the game is to kick the ball, encourage him to try. He can kick, and you can retrieve. Learning to kick a ball takes a great deal of balance and coordination. Be patient. After your toddler learns how to kick a stationary ball, recite the nursery rhyme to signal him when he is to kick the ball. To do this, the child stands in front of the ball and then on the word "Go!" he kicks it.

Finale

Young toddlers enjoy the same kinds of soft, small lightweight balls that are appropriate for infants. In addition, they like large rubber balls and beach balls. Show the toddler that when you drop a ball it will bounce up and down on the floor. Let him try it. Do not expect that your toddler will be able to catch a bouncing ball. That will come much later. Just show your toddler that if he drops a ball on the floor, it will bounce back up. Let your toddler experiment with bouncing a ball. (The best kind of ball for this age is a beach ball because it is soft and will not bounce too far.) After the toddler has had practice letting the beach ball bounce, introduce other age-appropriate balls such as foam balls and large rubber balls. (A table tennis ball or tennis ball rolling around inside a Frisbee™ will give your toddler moments of pleasure, too.)

Encore

Balls are probably the single most popular toy for toddlers. Balls bounce and they roll. Sometime between the ages of one and two, most toddlers become interested in a true game of catch. The easiest way to play catch with a toddler is to sit on the floor, facing each other with legs spread apart. Roll the ball back and forth so that it stays between your outstretched legs. Hallways are also good places to play games of catch. A variety of balls may be used safely indoors:
- ◆ Paper wads
- ◆ Rolled-up socks
- ◆ Balls of yarn
- ◆ Table tennis balls
- ◆ Inflated balloons (only with adult supervision)

The Bear Went over the Mountain

The bear went over the mountain,
The bear went over the mountain,
The bear went over the mountain,
To see what he could see.

Overture

Toddlers love to climb into everything. Watch and you will see how quickly your toddler can move in a straight line. Whereas she used to go around things, now she will scale a sofa, slide down stairs on her belly, or crawl under a chair to get where she wants to be.

Performance

Play: To reinforce climbing and descending, play "The Bear Went over the Mountain."
What you will need: Stuffed bear or other soft toy, soft overstuffed chair or sofa that the toddler can scale
How to play: Recite the rhyme as you use your hands to "walk" the bear from the floor, up onto a soft sofa or chair, and place it on the back of the chair. Encourage your toddler to climb up and get it. Then ask her to bring the bear to you. Repeat several times.

Finale

Recite the nursery rhyme as you "walk" the bear up the side of the sofa, across the seat, and up the back to the top of the sofa. Then recite another version of the nursery rhyme replacing the word "bear" with the toddler's name.
Example:

> Erica went over the mountain,
> Erica went over the mountain,
> Erica went over the mountain,
> To look for her bear.

On other occasions, use the personalized version of the rhyme to have your toddler move in other ways. For example:

> Sarah went over the bed, . . . to see what she could see.
> Sarah went around the bed, . . . to see what she could see.

Encore

To help your toddler learn how to maneuver around, into, over, and under objects, set up an obstacle course with cardboard boxes, kitchen chairs, blankets, etc. Show your toddler how to crawl through the maze. Then let her explore the course at her own speed.

Hickety, Pickety

*Hickety, pickety, my black hen,
She lays good eggs for gentlemen. . . .*
—Traditional Rhyme

Overture

Watch your toddler when he is tired and wants to sit down. Often children this age will go until they are too tired to take another step and then they will just flop down flat on their fannies. Sitting down in a chair—maneuvering into something without being able to see it—is difficult for most toddlers.

Performance

Play: To practice sitting down and getting up from a child-sized chair, play "Hickety, Pickety."

What you will need: Large plastic egg covered with aluminum foil or gold foil wrapping paper, child-sized chair

How to play: Have your toddler sit in the chair and close his eyes. Hide the egg under the chair. Cluck like a hen. Then tell the toddler to check to see if he laid an egg. Soon the child will be clucking after sitting down. Each time, place the golden egg under the chair. Then ask, "Did you lay an egg?" Your toddler will get plenty of practice sitting down and jumping up from the chair.

Finale

Have your toddler sit in the chair and close his eyes. Then place the egg under his chair. Recite the above rhyme. When you finish, have him check to see if there is an egg under the chair. On other occasions, recite the rhyme while cooking or serving eggs to your toddler.

Encore

To further reinforce sitting down and getting up from a chair, play "Find the Egg." Have your toddler sit in a chair with his eyes closed. Hide a plastic egg in the room with a bit of the egg showing. Recite the rhyme. Then tell the toddler to open his eyes, jump up, retrieve the egg, and then sit back down in the chair. Repeat as many times as your toddler wants to play the game. Give him an opportunity to hide the egg for you to find.

Little Bird

Once I saw a little bird, come hop, hop, hop.
So I cried, "Little bird, will you stop, stop, stop?" . . .
—Traditional Rhyme

Overture

Watch your toddler, and you will see that although she moves in a variety of ways. She will rarely take both feet off the ground at once. Hopping is a difficult large motor skill to learn. Occasionally, she will still use her arms to help keep her balance while walking. Do not expect to see your toddler using her hands for much more than balancing.

Performance

Play: To practice hopping with both feet together, play "Little Bird."
What you will need: No special equipment is needed to play this game.
How to play: With feet together, demonstrate how to move with tiny hops like a bird. Hold her hands to help her get started. Make peeping sounds as you hop about the room. When she can hop without holding your hands, flap your arms like wings. (It may be too difficult for your toddler to move her arms while hopping.) Hop around like little birds. Hop inside. Hop outside. Hop to music.

Finale

After your toddler knows how to hop with feet together, introduce the rhyme. Use the rhyme to play a game. As you recite the verse, encourage your toddler to hop like a bird. When you say "hop, hop, hop," the toddler is to hop. When you say "stop, stop, stop," she is to stand still.

Encore

On other occasions, sing varied versions of the rhyme and hop like other animals. Examples:

Once I saw a little frog, . . . Will you stop, stop, stop? (*Squat and use arms like front legs, hop with back legs.*)

Once I saw a little bunny, . . . Will you stop, stop, stop? (*Squat and hop.*)

Once I saw a kangaroo, . . . Will you stop, stop, stop? (*Great big leaps with feet together.*)

Dance with a Pig

Come dance a jig
With a baby pig.

Overture

Watch your toddler trying to carry things around with her while she moves about. Since he still needs his hands and arms for good balance, it is often difficult for a toddler to carry objects.

Performance

Play: To reinforce carrying objects while walking/running, play "Dance with a Pig."

What you will need: Soft, stuffed toy pig (or a lunch-sized bag stuffed with newspapers and tied at the top with a rubber band, with a pig face drawn on it)

How to play: Place the pig on a chair, sofa, or table at the other end of the room. Demonstrate how to walk to the toy, pick it up, and dance a little jig. Demonstrate these steps several times until your toddler gets the idea. Then invite your toddler to do the same by saying, "Come dance a jig with a baby pig." Use the rhyme to signal the toddler to begin the game. Each time you say the rhyme, the toddler can get the pig and do a jig.

Finale

Set up the game with several objects from which your toddler is to choose. Recite versions of the rhyme, naming particular objects. See if your toddler can select and then "jig" with the objects you name. Begin slowly with only two or three things from which to choose. Later work up to five or six choices for the toddler.

Examples:

Come dance a jig
With your father's hat.

Come dance a jig
With your sister's teddy bear.

Come dance a jig
With your brother's socks.

Encore

Never hesitate to dance a jig. Moving freely in celebration of your body and feelings will be a good example for your toddler. You will teach your toddler that expressing joy by moving to music and exerting energy to release tension is fun and healthy.

Pick Up a Pin

See a pin and pick it up,
All the day you will have good luck. . . .
—Traditional Rhyme

Overture

Watch and you will see that your toddler's pincher grip is developing. However, stooping to retrieve tiny objects from the floor takes a great deal of eye-hand coordination and full body balance. Retrieving things from the floor—especially small objects—will take a lot of practice.

Performance

Play: To help your toddler learn how to bend over and pick up small objects from the floor, play "Pick Up a Pin."

What you will need: Clothespins, basket

How to play: Scatter clothespins around on the floor. Ask the toddler to help you pick up the "pins" and put them in a basket. Recite the nursery rhyme while your toddler looks for the clothespins and picks them up on her own. Do not place the clothespins in a pile; instead, distribute them randomly about the room. Encourage her to stoop to pick them up, rather than sitting down on the floor first.

Finale

Play a version of this game by placing a variety of things on the floor: plastic egg, wooden block, stuffed bear, ball, etc. Recite the rhyme, replacing the word "pin" with the name of an object. Have your toddler look for the item you name, retrieve it, and put it in a basket or bring it to you. Repeat until all of the items have been picked up. This is a great game to play to get your child to put toys in a toy box. On other occasions, place a variety of toys at one end of the room. Ask your toddler to get a particular toy and bring it to you. One at a time, send your toddler to retrieve each toy.

Encore

An outdoor version of this game can be played by naming objects that the toddler can pick up from the ground.

Using a basket with a handle, have your toddler pick up leaves to fill the basket. If interested, pick up large pebbles, enough to fill your pockets. If you can walk on the beach, pick up shells, too.

Jack and Jill

Jack and Jill went up a hill,
To fetch a pail of water.
Jack fell down and broke his crown,
And Jill came tumbling after.
—Traditional Rhyme

Overture...

Watch and you will see that often your toddler will undertake more than he can manage and will become frustrated. Taking on new obstacles is a means of self-definition for children this age. The more powerful your toddler feels physically, the more significant he will feel as a person.

Performance..

Play: To practice moving quickly by rolling over and over again, play "Jack and Jill."
What you will need: No special equipment is needed to play this game.
How to play: Lie on the floor with your arms straight down at your sides. Demonstrate to your toddler how to roll over and over sideways. Encourage your toddler to roll over and over. He may need you to push his body to help him get the feel for this awkward way of moving.

Finale...

Use the nursery rhyme to play an action game. As you recite the verse, demonstrate each action.
   Jack and Jill went up a hill, (*Pretend to walk up a hill.*)
   To fetch a pail of water. (*Pretend to carry a bucket down the hill.*)
   Jack fell down and broke his crown, (*Tumble to the ground.*)
   Jill came tumbling after. (*Roll over and over.*)
Use a personalized version of the rhyme by replacing "Jack" and "Jill" with your toddler's name and "Mommy."
Example:
   (Toddler's name) and Mommy went up a hill, (*Pretend to walk up a hill.*)
   To fetch a pail of water. (*Pretend to carry a bucket down hill.*)
   Mommy fell down and broke her crown, (*Tumble to the ground.*)
   (Toddler's name) came tumbling after. (*Roll over and over.*)

On other occasions when playing outside, look for a grassy area with a slight incline. Help your toddler roll down the hill. Make sure the incline is enough to make rolling easy but not great enough to cause your toddler to lose control.

Encore..

Many nursery rhymes can be adapted to action play including:
   Jack be nimble, Jack be quick,
   Jack jumped over the candlestick.
   (*Run and jump over something like a string or line of tape on the floor.*)

   Little Miss Muffet, sat on a tuffet,
   Eating her curds and whey.
   Along came a spider, and sat down beside her,
   And frightened Miss Muffet away.
   (*Perform each action mentioned—sit, pretend to eat, jump up, run away.*)

End over End

End over end, head over heels,
Somersaulting like a wheel.

Overture

Watch your toddler moving about, and you will see her testing her limits. Excitedly she may leap about, twirling in a circle until she is dizzy and falling to the ground in a heap. Toddlers watch the way others move and try to master those movements, too.

Performance

Play: To introduce or reinforce somersaulting, play "End over End."

What you will need: Soft padded rug or grassy area

How to play: Show your toddler how to squat down, tuck her chin under, and roll forward. Use your hands to guide her in a soft-landing-somersault. Practice until she understands how to move in a forward roll. Recite the nursery rhyme while your toddler somersaults. Play music while somersaulting.

Finale

Assist your toddler in moving in other interesting ways:

- Lie on the floor on your back. Place your toddler's tummy on your feet and hold her hands. Lift her gently off the floor. Slowly move your legs from side to side or back and forth in a rocking movement.
- Sit in a chair. Cross your legs. Place the toddler on your ankle and hold her hands. Lift her off the ground in an up-and-down movement.
- Hold your toddler on one hip and extending one arm, hold one of her hands. Wrap your other arm around her and dance to slow music.

Try to provide an opportunity for your toddler to play on a small, low trampoline. Gymnastics is also very good for practicing gross motor skills. Playgrounds with age-appropriate swings, slides, and jungle gyms will provide your toddler with good gross motor practice.

Encore

Play other lifting and wrestling games, too. Some game ideas include:

- Holding your toddler at the waist with both hands, lift her high into the air. Use words like "up" and "down" as you move her.
- Kneel on the floor and tuck your head down like a turtle inside its shell. When your toddler climbs on your back, move about like a turtle walking.
- Large stuffed animals can be used for wrestling games. Move the animal with your hands as if it is playing with the toddler.
- Wrestle your toddler like you are a large mama or papa bear.

Jack Be Nimble

Jack be nimble, Jack be quick.
Jack jump over the candlestick.
—Traditional Rhyme

Overture

Watching your little toddler bravely move across a playground to join children at play can be thrilling. His newfound mobility will enable him to explore his environment more fully, broadening his scope of play.

Performance

Play: To reinforce all of the gross motor movements you have been teaching your toddler, play "Jack Be Nimble."

What you will need: No special equipment is needed for this game.

How to play: Demonstrate a movement the toddler has learned. Then have him copy that action. Include:

◆ Walk (in place)
◆ Tumble down
◆ Roll over
◆ Sit (in a chair)
◆ Climb (onto a sofa)
◆ Kick (a large ball)
◆ Reach (up to the sky)
◆ Pull (pull a toy)
◆ Push (push a toy)

Finale

Use a personalized version of the rhyme to review gross-motor actions.
Example: (Toddler's name), (toddler's name), followed by any of these:

◆ (Toddler's name) kick the ball over the fence.
◆ (Toddler's name) climb on the sofa.
◆ (Toddler's name) somersault in the grass.
◆ (Toddler's name) reach up to the sky.

Encore

Most toddlers love to be chased. Play a game of chase, and when you catch him, scoop him up and swing him around. Another variation: chase him and when you catch him, trap him between your legs, hold him by one foot, or wrestle him to the ground. Then let your toddler chase you. End the chasing games with hugs.

Keeping Track

Milestone	Date	Comments
Can walk alone		
Can pull a toy behind her		
Can run		
Can stand on tiptoes		
Can kick a large, stationary ball		
Can climb onto furniture		
Can climb down from furniture		
Can sit and get up from a child-sized chair		
Can hop with feet together		
Can carry objects while walking		
Can stoop and pick up objects		
Can roll over and over		
Can turn somersaults		

"No!" and "Why?"

Language Development

Contemplate

One of the most obvious changes in children this age is language acquisition. At twelve months, most babies are just uttering their first words. By the end of the second year, toddlers experience vocabulary spurts referred to as "name explosion." Toddlers suddenly learn as many as nine words per day. Toddlers quickly learn that when they say a word, it refers to a particular thing out there in the world. Toddlers also learn that when you point to, handle, or look at an object and say a word, you are naming a particular object. Once that important connection is made, language acquisition moves forward in leaps and bounds.

Language ability at this age varies greatly. Although some toddlers have a limited vocabulary, others have not yet spoken their first words. There is a tremendous variance in the age at which toddlers begin to say recognizable words. However, between 18 and 24 months, toddlers understand a great deal of what they hear. A lot of a toddler's messages will be nonverbal communication. He will make sounds to attract your attention and utter recognizable syllables like "mama" and "dada" to indicate family members.

Some toddlers begin to talk and then seem to hesitate and have trouble saying certain words. Should this happen, you can be helpful by simply waiting for your child to speak the word. Do not rush him. Do not correct him. Show your child that you are interested in what he is trying to say, but do not attempt to help him say it. The best way to help your toddler acquire language is to play some of the games that are provided in this section.

Language Development Milestones: 18 to 24 Months

- ◆ Will pay attention to speech and know when to answer a question
- ◆ Will understand when told "No"
- ◆ Will understand when told "Hot!"
- ◆ Will respond to simple verbal requests
- ◆ Will shake head for "no" and nod for "yes"
- ◆ Will address family members with pet names ("Mama," "Papa," "Sissy")
- ◆ Will use exclamations such as "Oh!"
- ◆ Will understand what many words mean
- ◆ Will make associations between objects and their names
- ◆ Will greet people with "Hello," "Hi," etc.
- ◆ Will imitate words that he hears
- ◆ Will understand that questions have answers
- ◆ Will understand some common action words
- ◆ Will understand that not all words are objects but rather that some describe objects

General Tips

It is believed that girls often develop language skills more quickly than boys. During the toddler years, some children master words, while others hardly speak at all. Do not be alarmed if your toddler seems slow in developing language skills. Encourage all of your toddler's attempts to speak by being a patient listener. If you seem bored, anxious, or irritated waiting for your child to find the right word, she will hesitate to try to communicate. Remember, it takes great skill to pull a word out from the stream of speech. Then the child has to connect the objects, actions, and events that go with the words she hears.

The best way to help your toddler advance her language development is to talk to her. As the day progresses, explain what is happening around her. Picture books can introduce and reinforce many words. When talking to your toddler, give plenty of opportunities for her to reply or to join in the conversation.

Gradually your toddler's words will begin to add a new dimension to her interactions with the world. She will even begin to refer to things that are not present and people who are absent. A child's speech is experimental, and she will test to see how those around her respond. When a toddler's language meets with great approval and acceptance, she will be anxious to keep talking. However, if words are corrected, misunderstood, or ignored the toddler will not be eager to

communicate in this new way. When you cannot understand your toddler's words, look for visual clues such as where she is looking or pointing. Smile a lot. Acknowledge every attempt your toddler makes to communicate. It might help to keep a good perspective on this time by imagining what it would be like for you to be in a foreign country where you could not speak even a single word. When you realize that your child is being introduced to many new words every day, her language acquisition is really very extraordinary.

Learning to listen effectively requires much training. When your toddler struggles to learn language, it may take a great deal of time to form each thought. Do not rush to fill in the missing words for her. Allow her the opportunity to speak her thoughts. If she talks too fast, slow her down by slowly repeating what you think you heard her say. When you listen patiently and interpret accurately, the child learns that her thoughts are important to you, and she will have the added benefit of watching you model good listening skills. Your child will feel as important as you treat her—treat her like a princess.

Sooo Big!

How big is baby?
Sooo big!

Overture

Watch your toddler's language development and you will see a remarkable transformation. While a one-year-old points and cries, an eighteen-month-old will often put his desires into words.

Performance

Play: To help your toddler learn how to respond to a question, play "Sooo Big!"
What you will need: No special equipment is needed to play this game.
How to play: Ask the toddler, "How big are you?" Then spread your hands far apart in an out-reached position and say, "Sooooooo big!" Repeat the sequence several times. Then when you ask the question, wait for your toddler to show how big he is with his own arms. As a bonus, he may begin to say the words "so big."

Finale

Use the rhyme to ask how big other people are. "How big is Brother? So big!" or "How big is Daddy?" Name family members, neighbors, and friends of the family and ask how big they are. Always tell the toddler he is "so big." On other occasions, after the toddler is very familiar with the game, ask new questions that sometimes require a "so little" response. Place your hands close together to indicate small objects.
Examples:
How little is Kitty?—So little.
How little are your toes?—So little.
How big is Daddy's car?—So big!
How little is this marshmallow?—So little.

Encore

Another game played with the hands and fingers is called "Houses." Recite the following finger play:
Here is a nest for the robin, (*Cup both hands.*)
Here is a hive for the bee, (*Fist together.*)
Here is a hole for the bunny, (*Finger and thumb make a circle.*)
And here is a house for me. (*Hold fingertips together to make a roof.*)
—*Author Unknown*

No! Go!

On the green light you go; but you stop on the red.
Freeze and don't move until "Go, green" is said.

Overture...

Listen to your toddler, and you may hear one particular word spoken many times each day: "No!" Although she may not seem to understand the meaning of the word when she is told "No," she will certainly expect you to understand what she means when she tells you "No!"

Performance...

Play: To reinforce the word "no" and help your toddler understand when told "No," play "No! Go!"

What you will need: No special equipment or toys are needed to play this game.

How to play: Demonstrate how to move on the word "go," and stop moving on the word "no." Say, "Go!" Move around, march, wave your arms, etc. Then say, "No," and freeze. Repeat until your toddler gets the idea. Then say the words "go" and "no" as the toddler moves and freezes at appropriate times.

Finale ....

Use the rhyme to learn the words "stop" and "go," too. Play little running games outside. Instead of saying "No" when you want the toddler to freeze, say "Stop." Introduce little red and green stoplights drawn on cardboard for racing. Always say "Go" when holding up the green sign. Say, "Stop" when holding up the red sign. On other occasions, use the rhyme to drink milk. As the toddler is drinking her milk, say, "Green light—go" or "Red light—stop." You can also use the color stoplights you have created to play this game as your toddler is drinking milk.

Encore ....

Toddlers communicate with their bodies rather than through vocalization. With only a small vocabulary, they must rely on their gestures, unique sounds, and jargon to express themselves. A favorite game for toddlers is touching an object with an index finger and trying to name it. The words a toddler learns will help her separate the objects in her world into categories: animals, foods, toys, etc. Place some toys on a table or the floor. As your toddler touches each one, ask, "Is this a bear?" Ask questions that she can answer with a shake or nod of her head or a verbal "yes" or "no." During the day, when you see your toddler touch an object, name the object.

Hot! Cold!

Pease-porridge hot,
Pease-porridge cold,
Pease-porridge in the pot,
Nine days old.
—Traditional Rhyme

Overture

Observe your toddler's speech. List the new words you hear him speak. As a toddler nears the age of two, he may learn as many as nine new words a day. At this age, toddlers learn that when they say a word, it refers to a particular object and that speaking gets them what they want.

Performance

Play: To help your toddler learn the words "hot" and "cold," play "Hot! Cold!"
What you will need: Warm mug of hot chocolate, glass of iced juice
How to play: Place the warm mug of hot chocolate and the glass of iced juice on a table. Hold your toddler in your lap. Demonstrate how to use one finger to touch the outside of each container. (Make sure the hot chocolate mug is not hot enough to burn a fingertip.) As you touch the warm mug with a fingertip, say, "Hot." Then touch the glass of juice and say, "Cold." Repeat several times. Holding the child's hand in yours, help him touch each one. Say the appropriate word each time he touches a container. After the hot chocolate has cooled a little, have the child taste each one and say the appropriate words.

Finale

Use the nursery rhyme to play "Pease-Porridge Hot." Put warm oatmeal and chilled oatmeal in bowls with milk and sugar. Feed your toddler small portions of each one as you recite the rhyme. Example:

Pease-porridge hot, (*Taste the warm oatmeal.*)
Pease-porridge cold, (*Taste the chilled oatmeal.*)
Pease-porridge in the pot, (*Clap, clap, clap.*)
Nine days old. (*Clap, clap, clap.*)

Encore

When telling stories or reading nursery rhymes that include foods, follow up with a tasting time. Examples:

◆ *The Tale of Peter Rabbit*—Blackberries, lettuce, French beans
◆ *The Gingerbread Man*—Gingerbread or gingersnap cookies
◆ *Goldilocks and the Three Bears*—Oatmeal
◆ *Winnie the Pooh*—Honey and bread
◆ "Hot Cross Buns"—Warm, sweet buns
◆ "Peter, Peter, Pumpkin-Eater"—Pumpkin pie
◆ "Sing a Song of Sixpence"—Pie or bread and honey

Hand Me the Shoe

Doodle doodle doo,
The Princess lost her shoe. . . .
—Traditional Rhyme

Overture

Watch your toddler, and you will see that not only can she ask for what she wants, her new mobility will make it possible for her to retrieve what she wants.

Performance

Play: To help your toddler learn how to respond to simple verbal requests, play "Hand Me the Shoe."

What you will need: Three familiar objects such as: your toddler's shoe, teddy bear, and a large silk flower

How to play: Place the objects on the floor between you and your toddler. Demonstrate by saying, "Here is the bear" and handing your toddler the bear. Then take the bear and place it on the floor again. Next, say, "Here is the shoe" and hand your toddler the shoe. Continue handing the child objects that you name and replacing each on the floor. If your toddler does not want to give up an object, say, "Hand me the teddy bear." Play with this concept until your toddler understands the directions. Extend the game by saying, "Put the teddy bear on the floor" or "Put the shoe in my lap."

Finale

Use a new rhyme to play a hide-and-seek game. Hide the three objects used in the "Hand Me the Shoe" game around the room. Be sure each one is only partially hidden. Demonstrate to the toddler how to look for the shoe, bear, and flower hidden around the room. Recite the new rhyme as you and your toddler search for the items. On other occasions, use a personalized version of the rhyme while looking for your toddler's shoes when getting dressed.
Example:

Doodle doodle doo,
(Toddler's name) lost her shoe.
Her Highness hopped—
And Mommy stopped,
Not knowing what to do.

Encore

Toddlers are avid explorers of wastebaskets, drawers, cabinets, and closets. Purses and briefcases are especially inviting, too. The adventurous and repetitive behavior of eighteen-month-olds helps them to remember where objects in their homes belong and where they are kept. Reinforce simple commands by asking your toddler to get things or put things away.

- ◆ Please bring your ball to me.
- ◆ Please put these socks on your bed (in the drawer, etc.).
- ◆ Please bring my hat to me.
- ◆ Please find your dolly and bring it to me.
- ◆ Please put Daddy's socks in the hamper.

Shake and Nod

*If "yess's" were "no's," and "no's" were "yess's,"
We would live with a lot of "guesses."*

Overture

As your toddler actually begins talking, you will respond by talking to him more, and thus his ability to communicate will flourish.

Performance

Play: To help your toddler learn how to shake his head for "no" and nod for "yes," play "Shake and Nod."

What you will need: Three toys with names that your toddler recognizes. Examples: bear, block, book.

How to play: Line up three toys on the floor between you and your toddler. Holding the bear, ask, "Is this a bear?" Nod your head and say, "Yes, this is a bear." Ask, "Is this a book?" Shaking your head say, "No, this is not a book; it is a bear." Repeat using the three items. Soon your toddler will be shaking or nodding his head when you ask the questions. Play until the toddler knows the objects well.

Finale

To teach your toddler the names of other objects, play a variation of this game. Line up three objects that go together, such as tools for self-care, fruits, or clothing. Examples: toothbrush, comb, soap; apple, banana, orange; or shoe, shirt, hat. As you hold up each object and ask a question, encourage the toddler to answer with a shake or nod of his head.

Encore

On other occasions, use a variation of this game to help your toddler recall objects without seeing them. Whether the toddler nods "yes," shakes his head for "no," or if he does not know the answer, reinforce the question and answer by verbalizing the appropriate response.
Examples:

Is Daddy big? (*Show big by spreading your hands out far apart in front of you. Say, "Yes, Daddy is big."*)

Is Mommy big? (*Show big by spreading your hands out far apart in front of you. Say, "Yes, Mommy is big, too."*)

Is puppy big? (*Show small by spreading your hands close together in front of you. Say, "No, puppy is not big."*)

Is the house big? (*Show big by spreading your hands out far apart in front of you. Say, "Yes, the house is big." Go outside and look at the house.*)

Is the car big? (*Show big by spreading your hands out far apart in front of you. Say, "Yes, the car is big." Go outside and look at the car.*)

Does (toddler's name) like milk? (*Say, "Yes, (toddler's name) likes milk."*)

Does (toddler's name) take naps? (*Say, "Yes, (toddler's name) takes naps."*)

Is this the kitchen? (*Say, "No, this is the living room." Go look at the kitchen.*)

Hello, Mother

Hello, Father; Hello, Mother.
Hello, Sister; Hello, Brother.

Overture......................................

Listen and make a list of the words your toddler can speak. In the next few months she will master many new words to be added to the list.

Performance..............................

Play: To encourage your toddler to address family members "Mama," "Papa," "Sissy," or whatever pet names she uses, play "Hello, Mother."

What you will need: Recent photographs of each member of the immediate family

How to play: Place the photographs on the floor between you and your toddler. Hold up a photograph and say, for example, "Hello, Mother." Use the name your toddler uses for each person in the family. After demonstrating how to greet the faces, hold up a photograph and let the toddler try.

Finale ....

Use the rhyme when Father or your toddler's siblings come home. Recite the rhyme and then, with great fanfare, announce who is home. For example: "Hello, Sissy." On other occasions, use photographs of extended family to familiarize your toddler with people she does not see everyday. Use only a few (two to four) photographs to play the game. Do not overwhelm the toddler with people she does not know or has never met. Play the game as you did with family members, naming each one and greeting them with a "Hello!" As an alternative version of the game, go around the house greeting objects that the toddler can name. Examples: "Hello, Bear" or "Hello, Bed."

Encore ....

It is never too early to begin reading to your child. The following are books written especially for toddlers and designed to teach very basic words.
- ◆ *My First Word Board Book* by Angela Wilkes (DK Pub. Merchandise, 1997)
- ◆ *Early Words* by Richard Scarry (Random House, 1976)
- ◆ *Baby's First Words* (A Chunky Book) by Lars Wik (Random House,1985)
- ◆ *This Is Me* (A Chunky Book) by Lenore Blegvad (Random House, 1985)
- ◆ *Baby Talk: Featuring Jim Henson's Sesame Street Muppets* (Sesame Street Books) by Linda Hayward (Random House, 1995)

Oh, Dear!

Oh, dear, what can the matter be?
This doesn't look right to me!

Overture..

Watch, and you will see that your toddler can not only name objects, but sometimes he will express his feelings with words. A blurted out exclamation will give you a very good clue about what he is feeling.

Performance...

Play: To encourage your toddler to use exclamations, play "Oh, Dear!"
What you will need: Pair of toddler's socks, shoes, mittens, hat
How to play: Place the socks, shoes, mittens, and hat on the floor between you and your toddler. Put a mitten on his foot and ask, "Oh, dear, what can the matter be?" Let the toddler take off the mitten if he can. Put the mitten on the toddler's hand and say something like: "Oh, good! It fits!" Next, put the other mitten on your thumb. Ask, "Oh, dear, what can the matter be?" If your toddler is interested, he can pull the mitten off your thumb. Place it on his other hand. Continue as follows:

1. Place a sock on your head and ask, "Oh, dear, what can the matter be?" Then put the sock on one of your toddler's feet. "Oh, good! It fits!"
2. Place a sock on the toddler's head and ask, "Oh, dear, what can the matter be?" Then place the sock on the toddler's other foot. "Oh, good! It fits!"
3. Place your toddler's hat on your head and ask, "Oh, dear, what can the matter be?" Then put the hat on the toddler. "Oh, good! It fits!"
4. Place one of your toddler's shoes on your thumb and ask, "Oh, dear, what can the matter be?" Then place the shoe on the toddler. "Oh, good! It fits!"
5. Place the other shoe on your head and ask, "Oh, dear, what can the matter be?" Then put the last shoe on the toddler. "Oh, good! It fits!"

Finale ....

Use the first line of the rhyme, and play with three other items of your own clothing, such as a hat, apron, and shoe. Use the same game rules to see if your toddler recognizes appropriate ways for you to wear each item.

Encore ....

On other occasions, use a personalized version of the nursery rhyme to encourage your toddler to do chores or comply.
Examples:

> Oh, dear, what can the matter be?
> (Child's name) toys are on the floor.
> This doesn't look right to me.

How I Wonder What You Are

Twinkle, twinkle, little star,
How I wonder what you are! . . .
—Traditional Rhyme

Overture

Observe your toddler's interest in naming objects. As she proudly points to and names objects, verbally praise her. As she learns the names of more and more things, it will give her a sense of accomplishment and a way of learning even more words.

Performance

Play: To help your toddler connect objects with their names, play "How I Wonder What You Are."
What you will need: Five or six familiar objects with easy-to-say names such as: bear, spoon, comb, book, shoe, ball
How to play: Place the objects on the floor between you and your toddler. Pick up an object and name it—"Bear." Then place the teddy bear back on the floor. One at a time, repeat with each object. Randomly pick up an object and name it—"Shoe." Soon your toddler will try to help name some of the objects. If she points to an object and tries to name it, pick it up and affirm her attempt. Repeat the names of the objects you hold several times. Play the game with the same objects for a few days, until your toddler can associate the name of each object with the actual object. This should be fun, not a quiz to test her knowledge.

Finale

Use the rhyme to learn the names of unfamiliar objects. When saying the two lines before naming an object, you are alerting your toddler to the game you are playing. It will get her attention and prepare her to hear a special word.

- ◆ When shopping, hold up a new and unfamiliar object such as a scrubber and say, "I wonder what you are." Then name the object— "Scrubber."
- ◆ When visiting a zoo, introduce the names of the animals in the same way.
- ◆ While shopping in a supermarket, name unfamiliar fruits and vegetables.

Encore

On other occasions, use the whole first verse of the song when outdoors at night. Look up at the stars and recite the rhyme or sing the song. Your awe of the night sky will teach your toddler to see boundless beauty, too.

Twinkle, twinkle, little star,
How I wonder what you are!
Up above the world so high,
Like a diamond in the sky.

Hello!

"Salutations are greetings," said the voice.
When I say 'salutations,' it's just my fancy way
of saying hello or good morning."
—Charlotte's Web by E. B. White

Overture

Actions and the thoughts your toddler has about them will come before he can say the words. That is why it is educational to involve your toddler in a lot of actions that you name for him. For example, when you say "Hello," wave your hand. When you say "I love you," give him a hug.

Performance

Play: To encourage the toddler to greet people with "Hello," "Hi," or his greeting of choice, play "Hello!"

What you will need: No equipment is needed to play this game.

How to play: Carry your toddler around and greet familiar things in the house with words and actions. While waving, name objects and say "Hello" or whatever greeting is preferred by your toddler. Examples:

"Hello, clock."
"Hello, teddy bear."
"Hello, bed."

After playing the game for a while, have the toddler say the greeting while you add the name of the object. Use the same game to greet objects in the yard. Take a hike and greet the trees, grass, sun, clouds, flowers, squirrels, etc. Name the familiar outside objects for your toddler so he can see the objects while hearing the words.

Finale

On other occasions, play the game by waving and saying "Good night" or "Good-bye" to objects before going to bed or when leaving the house. Examples:

"Good night, bear."
"Good-bye, house."
"Good-bye, tricycle."

Encore

Toddlers must be taught about not greeting strangers. The goal is to educate your child without making him fearful. Explain what a stranger is. Assure your toddler that it is okay to chat with strangers when he is beside you. Caution him that it is not okay to talk to strangers when he is alone or with other children. Assure him that most people truly care for children and would not hurt him; warn him that a few people are not friends and are not safe.

Say What I Say

Baa, baa, black sheep,
Have you any wool? . . .
—Traditional Rhyme

Overture ....

Watch your toddler when you speak to her. Often she will be watching you form words. She will be listening to the sounds you make. She will try to imitate the sounds she hears even when she does not know the meaning of the words.

Performance ....

Play: To encourage the toddler to imitate sounds that she hears, play "Say What I Say."
What you will need: Nothing is needed to play this game.
How to play: Hold your toddler in your lap. Then say, "Say what I say" and make a one-syllable sound such as "ma." Wait for your toddler to make the sound. If she does not understand what you want her to do, repeat the sound yourself. Repeat it until your toddler tries to make the sound, too. Then say, "Say what I say" and make a new sound. Easiest-to-say sounds include the short vowel "a" and long vowel "e" proceeded by the consonant sound for "b," "d," "m," "p," or "t." Some examples include:

ba (sound a lamb makes)	be (sound in beetle)
da (sound in daughter)	de (sound in deep)
ma (sound in mama)	me (sound in meat)
pa (sound in papa)	pe (sound in peek)
ta (sound in talk)	te (sound in tea)

Tell your toddler, "Say what I say." Then make one of the sounds. No matter what response you get, say something like, "That is very good. You make wonderful sounds." Repeat using all of the sounds.

Finale ....

Use another version of the rhyme to introduce these same sounds in a new way. Play with the sounds. Make a new sound, and have the toddler make the sound used in the rhyme.
Examples:
Baa, baa, black sheep. What did I say? (Toddler says "baa.")
Bee, bee, bumble bee. What did I say?
Tea, tea, hot tea. What did I say?
Me, me, look at me. What did I say?
Da, da, he's my daddy. What did I say?

Encore ....

As you go about your work in the house, make playful sounds. Your toddler should hear all sorts of sounds including: whispers, whistles, singing, cooing, babbling, honking, etc. Use cardboard tubes to make sounds more intriguing. Soon your toddler will be using the cardboard tubes to amplify her sounds, too.

"What Do They Call You?"

What do they call you?
What's your name?

Overture

Listen to what your toddler has to say about things. He needs to know that when he talks to people, they are ready to listen and willing to respond. When you ask your toddler a question and then listen carefully to his answer, it sends him a clear message that you care about his thoughts.

Performance

Play: To help your toddler begin to answer questions, play "What Do They Call You?"
What you will need: Five or six stuffed toys with names
How to play: Place the stuffed toys on the floor between you and your toddler. Pick up a toy and ask, "What do they call you? What's your name?" Then name the stuffed toy in a question so the toddler can nod or say "Yes."
Examples:

- ◆ What do they call you? What's your name? Is your name Raggedy Ann?
- ◆ What do they call you? What's your name? Is your name Mr. Bear?
- ◆ What do they call you? What's your name? Is your name Jingles the Clown?
- ◆ Point to your toddler and ask, "What do they call you? What's your name? Is your name (toddler's name)?"

Continue asking the question ("What do they call you? What's your name?") and phrasing the answers as questions ("Is your name Raggedy Ann?"). Your toddler can answer with a nod. The object is not to learn to speak the words but to hear how questions are phrased and to know that questions require an answer.

Finale

Use the same stuffed toys and play another version of this game. Turn it into a guessing game. Ask the same questions, but sometimes give a wrong name for one of the stuffed toys. For example, while holding Mr. Bear, you might ask, "What do they call you? Is your name Raggedy Ann?" Your toddler has an opportunity to shake his head or say "no."

Encore

On other occasions, use the questions when looking at photograph albums of family members. Point to a photograph, ask the questions, then name the person in the form of a question.
Examples:

- ◆ What do they call you? What's your name? Are you Uncle Andy?
- ◆ What do they call you? What's your name? Are you Grandma Lamb?
- ◆ What do they call you? What's your name? Are you Cousin Crystal?

Pat the Bunny

Pat the bunny, touch the dog.
Hug the kitty, kiss the frog.

Overture

Toddlers learn words more quickly when they can associate them with objects or actions. Demonstrating an action word will help your toddler grasp its meaning.

Performance

Play: To introduce and reinforce common action words for your toddler, play "Pat the Bunny."
What you will need: It is best if you have the following stuffed or plastic toys: bunny, dog, kitty, and frog. If you cannot obtain a stuffed bunny, dog, kitty, and frog, substitute four other stuffed animals and change the rhyme accordingly.
How to play: Place the animals on the floor between you and the toddler. Say, "Pat the bunny" and demonstrate. One at a time, pat each animal as you repeat the phrase "pat the bunny (dog, kitty, frog)." Then tell the toddler which animal to pat. Be flexible. Your toddler may get distracted and want to play with one of the toys. Encourage playing the game by asking your toddler to pat each animal.

Finale

Use the rhyme and the appropriate stuffed animals to demonstrate the following actions: pat, touch, hug, and kiss. For this game, your toddler will not only be practicing the name for each animal, she will be learning action words, too. On other occasions, use revised versions of this rhyme to include names of other toys and additional actions, such as point to, hold, squeeze, feel, pick up, snuggle, cuddle, etc.

Encore

Some basic words that should become part of your toddler's speech are listed below. Use these descriptive words plus others that you know.
  Hot/Cold—The stove is hot; the refrigerator is cold.
  Slow/Fast—The snail is slow; the car is fast.
  Stop/Go—Stop! Do not go across the street.
  Over/Under—The sky is over us; the grass is under us.
  Full/Empty—The carton is full; the box is empty.
  Large/Small—The house is large; the bug is small.
  Open/Shut—Open the door; shut the door.
  Boy/Girl—Brother is a boy; sister is a girl.
  Round/Square—The ball is round; the book is square.
  Down/Up—Go down the stairs; go up the stairs.
  Quiet/Loud—The kitten's purr is quiet; the dog's bark is loud.

Which One?

As soft as silk, as big as a house.
As white as milk, as quiet as a mouse.

Overture

Connections between the nerves in the brain multiply rapidly between birth and age two. During this period toddlers can absorb information like sponges, but they have not yet developed the ability to fully process the incoming data and are sometimes overwhelmed by the onslaught of information.

Performance

Play: To help your toddler sort out descriptive words, play "Which One?"

What you will need: Objects to demonstrate descriptive words: empty (plastic cup), full (box full of something), soft (stuffed toy), hard (blocks), heavy (big book), light (scarf), loud (horn to blow), quiet (small stuffed kitten)

How to play: One at a time, pick up an object and name it with a descriptive word. Then hand it to the toddler. Repeat the description.

Examples:
◆ Empty cup/full box
◆ Soft bear/hard block
◆ Heavy book/light scarf
◆ Loud horn (blow it)/quiet kitty

Introduce the objects in pairs of opposites. Then place the objects back on the floor and introduce another set of opposites. If the toddler wants to hold and manipulate the objects, simply name and describe the ones he is holding or touching. Be flexible as the child chooses which objects to inspect. When your child is very familiar with the names of objects and descriptive words, hold up two objects and ask, "Which one is soft?" or "Which one is hard?" (Note, there may be more than one correct response. Example: a kitty is soft, light, quiet, and possibly full.) Encourage your toddler to hold or point to his choice. If the toddler does not understand the game, try using only one set of opposites at a time or save this activity for another day when your toddler is a few months older.

Finale

After your toddler is familiar with the descriptive words for each object, play the game a new way. Using the same objects again, describe an object and see if the toddler can choose an appropriate object from the group of objects. Remember, there may be many correct answers. For example, choosing the block for "quiet" is correct.

Encore

On other occasions, play "Let's Find Another One." Name and describe one of the objects. Then say, "Let's go find another toy that is quiet (loud, soft, heavy, etc.)" Look through the toys in your toddler's room. Keep asking the question, "Which ones are soft?" etc. Make a pile of soft things. Then choose a new adjective and sort through the toys to make a new pile.

Keeping Track

Milestone	Date	Comments
Pays attention to speech		
Knows when being asked a question		
Understands when told "No"		
Understands when told "Hot!"		
Responds to simple verbal requests		
Can shake head for "no" and nod for "yes"		
Addresses family members— "Mama," "Papa," "Sissy," etc.		
Uses exclamations such as "Oh!"		
Understands what many words mean		
Makes connections between objects and their names		
Can greet people with "Hello," "Hi," etc.		
Can imitate sounds heard		
Understands that questions have answers		
Understands common action words		
Understands common descriptive words		

What's That?

Cognitive Development

Contemplate

It is fascinating to watch the rapid development and behavioral changes that occur in toddlers. The extraordinary expansion of their play, thinking, talking, and socializing is due to tremendous brain growth. As your toddler grows, connections between the nerves in his brain multiply rapidly—especially during the second year. At this developmental stage, toddlers absorb information like sponges, but they do not have the ability to fully process all of the things they are learning; they can easily become overwhelmed by information. Go slowly while playing cognitive games with your toddler.

Watch and you will see your toddler becoming increasingly purposeful in his play. During the second half of the second year, toddlers are interested in pop-up boxes, shape sorters, form boards, simple puzzles, and complex nesting materials. If he does not already enjoy looking at books, your one-and-a-half-year-old will begin to spend time with them. For independent viewing, appropriate books for young toddlers include cloth, plastic, and cardboard books. Some children this age are ready for "touch and feel" and other tactile books with heavy paper pages. For lap reading with an adult, your toddler will need large picture books with only a few words or one line per page and nursery rhyme books. Your toddler will probably enjoy listening to simple rhymes.

Cognitive Development Milestones: 18 to 24 Months

◆ Will explore objects by shaking, banging, throwing, dropping
◆ Will be able to find hidden objects
◆ Will learn how to imitate a facial expression
◆ Will understand the function of a telephone
◆ Will learn to recognize and point out parts of the face and body
◆ Will begin to enjoy hearing short stories
◆ Will learn to recognize positions: "up," "down," "under," and "around"
◆ Will learn how to respond to his own name
◆ May begin to enjoy helping you perform simple household chores
◆ Will begin to pretend he is doing adult work
◆ Will learn how to use non-toy play materials with handles
◆ Will learn how to match identical objects
◆ Will learn how to distinguish between objects that are not alike

General Tips

During your toddler's second year of life, you will observe a remarkable intellectual transformation taking place. She will go from being a helpless baby to being a full-fledged person. A giant leap in knowledge occurs between a toddler's first and second birthday. The myriad of physical, emotional, and cognitive advances will change the way your toddler interacts with the world. One-and-a-half-year-olds have minds of their own. They have wants and needs and new ways to get these wants and needs fulfilled. Not only will the toddler begin to verbally express her desires, her mobility will allow her to go after what she wants, too.

As your child's cognitive abilities improve, she can think about things that she cannot see. Improved memory and problem-solving skills help a toddler act and move in goal-directed ways. She knows what she wants, and if she does not get it, she will plan a strategy of acquisition. As she learns to meet her own needs, she will want more and more independence. Do not label your toddler's need for independence as "defiant behavior." Becoming independent is your child's only path to becoming a whole person.

During the second half of her second year, books will take on new significance for your toddler. Books appropriate for young toddlers include those made from cloth, plastic, and cardboard. More fragile books may be used for lap reading with an adult. Choose large picture books with simple pictures and storybooks with just a few words or simple story line. Some books have no words, and the pictures tell the story. Children this age have a sense of wonder. Every day is an opportunity to learn new things and experience new games. Books are a great way to introduce toddlers to fanciful characters and interesting places.

There are materials your toddler needs for exploring her world. Cognitive development depends upon your toddler's ability to sort and classify objects. She will be mentally grouping every object she sees. In order for your toddler to expand her intellectual and creative horizons, you will need to broaden her experiences as much as possible. View your trips to the supermarket or shopping mall as scientific expeditions. Remember, everything your toddler sees will be new to her. She will find ordinary things quite extraordinary. Take your toddler to places in the neighborhood such as the fire station, police station, bakery, bank, and produce stand. Talk about everything she sees on these outings. Discuss the things your toddler sees while you are there and then again when you get home. Right now your toddler's brain is like a sponge, soaking up everything she experiences. The more rich her environment, the more knowledgeable about her world she can become.

Shake, Rattle, and Roll

Shake, rattle, and roll.
Shake, rattle, and rock!

Overture

What is fascinating about a toddler's intellectual development, is that it is closely tied to physiological changes occurring in his brain. The more sensory your toddler's games are, the more he will learn from the experiences.

Performance

Play: To encourage your toddler to explore objects by shaking, banging, throwing, and dropping, play "Shake, Rattle, and Roll."

What you will need: Four plastic bottles with handles, variety of beans or pasta shapes (split peas, broken spaghetti, lima beans), rice, white glue

How to play: Fill each plastic bottle with ¼ cup (59 ml) of a different kind of bean or pasta. Use white glue around the lid to make sure your toddler will not open the bottle. Let the glue dry. Demonstrate how to make a variety of sounds by shaking, rattling, and rolling the bottles. Let your toddler choose two rattles and you take the other two. Recite the rhyme and shake the rattles while moving about in the room.

Finale

Use a variety of household objects to make shakers. Be sure the lids are glued on securely so your toddler cannot take out the small objects.

- Fill plastic margarine containers with several spoons of chocolate chips.
- Fill plastic soda bottles half-full of dried miniature marshmallows.
- Fill square, gourmet coffee tins half-full of broken spaghetti noodles.
- Fill plastic bottles half-full of sand and pebbles.
- Fill a Styrofoam egg carton with rice and duct tape it shut.
- Put several marbles inside a spice can and securely tape it shut.

Take the quiet, more pleasant sounding rattles on trips in the car. They will amuse your child with a variety of sounds and keep his hands busy.

Encore

On other occasions, provide wooden spoons and other safe things for your child to bang against each other or on the floor. Make a clapping beat, and see if your toddler can begin to keep the beat with the banging instruments. If interested, play music for your toddler to accompany.

Peekaboo

Peekaboo!
I see you.

Overture

Watch your toddler, and you will see how fascinated she is with her own body. Games that emphasize the toddler as an individual, separate from her caregivers, will advance her self-esteem.

Performance

Play: To help your toddler learn how to find hidden objects, play "Peekaboo."
What you will need: Soft cloth or silk scarf
How to play: Drape a cloth or silk scarf over the toddler's head and ask, "Where is (toddler's name)?" Lift the scarf, act very surprised, and say, "There she is!" Repeat several times. Soon she will understand the game and pull the scarf away herself. Your toddler may think that if her head is covered, you cannot see any part of her body. Encourage the toddler to hide your head under the scarf. When she pulls off the scarf, say, "Peekaboo! I see you." When your toddler pulls the scarf off your head, say "Oh my, there you are! I wondered where you had gone."

Finale

Use the rhyme and play peekaboo by placing your toddler on her back, facing toward you. Lift both her legs together so that they conceal your face. Then open them wide and say, "Peekaboo! I see you." Repeat. Soon the toddler will understand the game and move her own legs and feet. This is a good game to play while diapering. On other occasions, play another version of peekaboo by hiding behind a door or furniture. Place your foot, arm, or nose in your toddler's view. Say, "Peekaboo!" See if your toddler can find you.

Encore

Try playing peekaboo games in front of a full-length mirror. Sit so you and your toddler can see yourselves in the mirror. Hold up a towel or small blanket between you and your toddler so that she cannot see you but can still see your image in the mirror. Say, "Peekaboo." Watch to see what your toddler does:

- Does she lift the towel and look under it?
- Does she peek around the towel without moving it?
- Does she pull the towel down to see your face?
- Does she look at your reflection in the mirror and not touch the towel at all?

Play a variation of this game; "find" your toddler using all of the above methods.

Make This Face

*Tommy's tears and Mary's fears
Will make them old before their years.*
—Traditional Rhyme

Overture

You may not be aware of it, but your toddler is always watching you for nonverbal clues. If you are angry, even if you do not speak cross words, your toddler knows by your face. Watch your toddler closely, and you will see that he is often watching you for signs of your emotional state.

Performance

Play: To encourage the toddler to imitate a gesture, play "Make This Face."

What you will need: Plastic hand mirrors

How to play: Give the toddler a hand mirror or hold a hand mirror so he can see into it. Make a face in the mirror. Tell your toddler, "Make this face." Look at the face he makes in the mirror. Try these facial expressions:

◆ Scrunch up your nose.
◆ Make a big smile.
◆ Make a sleepy face.
◆ Pout.
◆ Open your mouth for a surprised look.
◆ Pretend to cry, "Boo hoo."
◆ Put on a cross look.

Finale

Play a game of imitating a face made by the other person. Say something like this: "Can you make this sad face?" or "Can you make a big happy face?" Demonstrate and verbally describe each face, and see if your toddler can make the face, too. Praise his every attempt to make the same facial expression.

Encore

On other occasions, experiment with painting faces.

◆ Sit the toddler in his high chair and place a plastic mirror on the tray. Using finger paints, let your toddler paint his reflection that he sees in the mirror.
◆ Use face paints to paint a face on your toddler. Let him see his new face in a mirror.
◆ Paint a clown face on your own face. See if your toddler likes it.
◆ With fine-tip watercolor markers, draw a butterfly or flower on your toddler's hand or foot.

Telephone

Ring, ring! Answer the phone.
Hello, hello. Who is this?

Overture

When talking to your toddler, props such as a play telephone, microphone, and tape recorder are good toys for developing cognitive skills.

Performance

Play: To help your toddler learn how to talk on the telephone, play "Telephone."
What you will need: A play telephone or a telephone that is not plugged in
How to play: After saying "Ring, ring," demonstrate how to lift the receiver. Say, "Hello." Then replace the receiver. Then say "Ring, ring" again and encourage your toddler to lift the receiver. Have a conversation, and pretend you are talking to the child through the telephone. Say, "Good-bye," and replace the receiver. Practice lifting the receiver on "ring, ring" and hanging up after saying "good-bye."

Finale

Use a new version of the rhyme, and play a game of answering a telephone, opening a door, or pretending to sleep. Praise your toddler highly when she performs the right action.
Examples:

Ring, ring! Answer the phone.
Hello, hello. Who is this? (*Pick up receiver.*)

Buzz, buzz! Answer the door.
Hello, hello. Do come in. (*Open a door.*)

Snore, snore. Go to bed.
Good night, good night. Sweet dreams. (*Close eyes and pretend to sleep.*)

Encore

Telephones are great motivators for teaching toddlers social skills, such as listening. On other occasions, use the telephone to help your toddler extend her vocabulary.

◆ Let the toddler listen to family and friends who call on the telephone.
◆ If you have more than one line in your house, call your toddler and talk to her on the telephone.
◆ Have Father or her siblings call your toddler when they are away from the house and ask her questions she can answer with "yes" and "no."
◆ Make sure your toddler has her own play telephone.

Brow Brinky, Eye Winky

Brow brinky; Eye winky,
Chin choppy; Nose noppy,
Cheek cherry; Mouth merry.
— Traditional Rhyme

Overture

Watch your toddler, and you will see that he is motivated when learning about his own body. He wants to know how his body works and is interested to find out what each body part can do.

Performance

Play: To help your toddler learn to name parts of the face, play "Brow Brinky, Eye Winky."
What you will need: No special equipment is needed for this game.
How to play: Use the rhyme to teach parts of the face: eyebrows, eyes, chin, nose, cheeks, and mouth. This game can be played in four different stages.

- Recite the verse as you point to the appropriate part of your face.
- Recite the verse while touching the appropriate place on the toddler's face.
- Recite the verse, and let your toddler point to the appropriate place on his face while you point to the appropriate part of your face.
- Recite the verse, and let the toddler point to the appropriate part of his face independently.

Finale

Sing the nursery rhyme to the tune: "Twinkle, Twinkle, Little Star." Encourage your toddler to touch the appropriate places on his face as you sing about each one. On other occasions, have the toddler touch other parts of his face and body.
Examples:

- Show me your tongue.
- Touch your ears.
- Blink your eyes.
- Touch your mouth.
- Touch your elbow.

- Touch your lips.
- Shake your hair.
- Please touch your nose.
- Touch your toes.

Encore

A body parts game can become livelier still if you make an unexpected sound when your toddler touches you. For example: Tell the toddler to squeeze your nose. When he does, quack like a duck. Try some of these:

- Pull chin—roar like a lion.
- Pull ears—crow like a rooster.
- Squeeze your cheeks—honk like a goose.
- Rub your head—purr like a kitten.
- Pat your head—bark like a dog.

Story Time

John, John, the preacher's son,
Learned to listen when he was young.

Overture

Watch your toddler while she is listening to a story, and you will know when she has heard enough. Although her attention span may be short, reading a story is often so interesting that it will help your toddler extend the amount of time she can sit quietly.

Performance

Play: To encourage your toddler to listen to stories, set up a regular "Story Time." Just before going to sleep each night is a good time to tell stories. The story can be read or told and only needs to last a minute or two. Story time should be something that happens every day—something your toddler can depend upon.

What you will need: Picture books

How to play: Large picture books with only a few words on each page are best. Sit with your toddler in your lap or snuggle her down in her bed. Hold the book in front of the child so she can see the pictures. Read slowly. Turn the pages when your toddler is completely finished looking at them. There is no need to rush; let her set the pace. Choose age-appropriate books including:
- *Goodnight Moon* by Margaret Wise Brown (HarperCollins Juvenile Books, 1991)
- *Corduroy* by Don Freeman (Viking Press, 1985)
- *A Snowy Day* by Ezra Jack Keats (Viking Press, 1962)
- *More More More Said the Baby: 3 Love Stories* by Vera B. Williams (Tupelo Books, 1997)

Finale

Use nursery rhyme books for story time. Recite a rhyme several times. Hold the toddler's hands and clap a rhythm while reciting the rhyme.

Encore

On other occasions, encourage your toddler's interest in books in a variety of ways.
- Visit the library and look at books.
- Find out if the library has a story time for toddlers.
- Let your toddler choose a book at a bookstore.
- Read to your toddler while you are waiting in the doctor's office.
- When you see someone reading in the park or other places, point out to your toddler that the person is reading a magazine, newspaper, book, etc.
- Make books special by handling them as treasures and giving them as gifts.
- Make sure your toddler sees you reading every day.

Driving Up, Driving Down

Driving up. Driving down,
Driving all around our town.

Overture

Learning and using prepositions is confusing for toddlers. You can help your toddler learn prepositions and words that describe relationships by using them often in activities and games.

Performance

Play: To help your toddler learn to recognize and point to positions "up," "down," "into," and "around," play "Driving Up, Driving Down."

What you will need: To play the game, you will need a cardboard box and toy cars. Cut large holes in each side of the box so you have a play garage that cars can enter and exit. Attach a cardboard ramp to the garage so the cars can drive up to get to the "roof" of the garage.

How to play: Place the cardboard garage and cars on the floor between you and your toddler. As you move a car, make statements that describe the position of the car.
Examples:
- I am driving "up" the ramp. Up.
- I am driving "down" the ramp. Down.
- I am driving "under" the ramp. Under.
- I am driving "around" the garage. Around.
- I am driving "into" the garage. Into.

Finale

Recite the rhyme as you and your toddler play with cars. Use toy cars and the cardboard box in a sandbox. As your toddler is moving the car, describe what he is doing.
Examples:
- You are driving "up" the ramp. Up.
- You are driving "down" the ramp. Down.
- You driving "under" the ramp. Under.

On other occasions, use the rhyme when driving around town in the car. Say things like:
- We are driving "up" the hill. Up.
- We are backing "out" of the driveway. Out.

Encore

Toddlers love to get inside containers. A large box, such as an appliance box, might become your toddler's second home. You can extend your toddler's play inside the box by pretending to knock on the door when you want to talk to him. Hand him paper and say something like: "Here is your mail." Other enclosed areas toddlers like to get inside or under include:
- Under or inside blanket tents
- Under beds with blankets hanging to the floor

Everybody's Fancy

Everybody's fancy, every body's fine.
Your body is fancy and so is mine.
—Fred Rogers

Overture

Watch and you will see your toddler's self-exploration becoming heightened. Your toddler will be intrigued with her own eyes, mouth, and ears. She will enjoy watching how her fingers and toes move.

Performance

Play: To help your toddler appreciate how "fancy" her body is, play "Everybody's Fancy."
What you will need: No special equipment is needed to play this game.
How to play: When talking to your toddler, use her name frequently. You can review body parts and reinforce the toddler's recognition of her own name as she points to the body parts you name. It is okay if she cannot point to the body part the first time. Demonstrate how to do it until your toddler can do it, too.
Examples:
Touch Amy's nose.
Touch Amy's toes.
Touch Amy's feet.
Touch Amy's knees.

Finale

Recite or sing a personalized version of the song.
Example:
(Toddler's name) is fancy,
(Toddler's name) is fine.
(Toddler's name)'s body is fancy
And so is mine.
On other occasions, add body parts to the song and sing it again.
Example:
(Toddler's name)'s arms are fancy,
(Toddler's name)'s arms are fine.
(Toddler's name)'s arms are fancy
And so are mine.

Encore

Cut pictures of your toddler's favorite animals, foods, and toys from magazines and mount them on heavy paper. Place the pictures around the room. Talk about them during the day. Help your toddler distinguish between pictures of objects and the real objects through discussions.
Example:
◆ Where is the *picture* of the red wagon? Where is your red wagon?
◆ Where is the *picture* of the dog? Where is our dog, Rags?

Spic-and-Span

Handy Spandy, Jack-a-dandy.
Cleans the kitchen, spic and spandy.

Overture

Watch your toddler's face when he is helping you. There is a great deal of pride associated with helping Mommy/Daddy. You can give your child an opportunity to feel worthwhile by giving him simple chores.

Performance

Play: To encourage the toddler to help with household chores, play "Spic-and-Span."
What you will need: Child-sized broom and dust rag
How to play: Using your own broom and dust rag, demonstrate how to sweep and dust furniture. Say something like: "I like to keep the house spic and span." Give your toddler the child-sized tools, and see if he wants to join in the cleaning. Ask, "Do you want to help keep the kitchen spic-and-span?" If your toddler wants to sweep or dust, praise every effort he makes.

Finale

Use the nursery rhyme when cleaning the kitchen. Substitute "Jack" with your toddler's name. On other occasions, invite your toddler to watch you. Simple chores that he will be able to perform now or when he is closer to three years old include:

- ◆ Washing and tearing large lettuce leaves for a salad
- ◆ Scrubbing vegetables with a brush
- ◆ Cutting cookies with a cookie cutter
- ◆ Placing letters in the mailbox
- ◆ Sorting socks by colors
- ◆ Clearing the table of unbreakable items
- ◆ Watering plants with a small watering can
- ◆ Folding small kitchen towels
- ◆ Picking up his toys

Encore

Although often motivating, cooking or preparing food represents some dangerous activities and should be saved until your toddler is older. However, doing the laundry includes several safe and simple tasks that your toddler can tackle. Toddlers can be responsible to put dirty clothes in a hamper. Sorting the laundry is another activity in which toddlers like to take part. Sorting dirty laundry into white and colored piles and then (standing on a sturdy chair) throwing the clothes into the washing machine is good practice for your toddler. It will take more time when you allow your toddler to help with household chores, but it will give your toddler a great deal of satisfaction and good feelings about being a contributing part of the family.

Wash the Dishes

This is the way we wash the dishes, wash the dishes, wash the dishes.
This is the way we wash the dishes, early in the morning.

Overture

Watch your toddler while she is playing in water, and you will see her making scientific discoveries. Since your toddler's language is limited, the way she learns most things will be by experiencing them. She may not have the vocabulary to understand "buoyancy," but through bathtub play she will learn to sort things that can float from things that sink.

Performance

Play: To encourage your toddler to see what kinds of things float and sink, play "Wash the Dishes."
What you will need: Plastic, toy dishes; dishrag and dish towels; tub of warm sudsy water; tub of warm rinse water
How to play: Place tubs of water in a sink or area where it is okay to splash. Place the plastic toy dishes near the tubs. Put one towel next to the tub where clean dishes may drain. Demonstrate how to wash the dishes in soapy water and rinse them in clean water. Then place them on a towel to drain. Demonstrate how to dry dishes. Give the child the dishrag, and invite her to help you wash the dishes. Supervise, so your child is safe with the water, but let the toddler do the "work."

Finale

Use the rhyme while washing dishes. Use various versions of the rhyme when the toddler helps you with other chores.
Example:

> This is the way we feed the cat,
> Feed the cat, feed the cat.
> This is the way we feed the cat,
> Early in the morning.

Encore

Picking up her own toys can become a great game, and at the same time, it will save you from bending over and picking them up. Making your toddler responsible for the care of her own toys is a good lesson that she is old enough to learn. Personalize the verse when your child is "working."
Example:

> This is the way (toddler's name) picks up toys,
> Picks up her toys, picks up her toys.
> This is the way (toddler's name) picks up her toys,
> Before she goes to bed.

Sweep and Dig

Sweep, sweep, sweep. Make it neat.
Dig, dig, dig. Make it deep.

Overture

Your toddler's expanded ability to use tools in correct ways reflect underlying brain growth. Watch and you will see that information he learns in one situation will sometimes be transferred when working at another task. This ability to apply learning to different situations will make your toddler's intellectual leap even greater.

Performance

Play: To reinforce the use of non-toy play, give your toddler toy tools with handles: a child-sized broom, mop, rake, shovel, etc. Use the tools to play "Sweep and Dig."
What you will need: Child-sized broom, mop, rake, and shovel
How to play: Demonstrate with a regular-sized broom, mop, shovel, and rake how to use each tool. One at a time, give your toddler the child-sized tool to mimic what you are doing. Examples: Sweep the porch. Mop the steps. Rake some leaves. Dig a hole. Then leave the toddler to pick and choose which tools he wants to use while you finish sweeping the porch or raking leaves.

Finale

Use another version of the nursery rhyme and the toy tools to play a guessing game. Line up the broom, mob, rake, and shovel. Recite a verse, and see if your toddler knows which tool is associated with the words in the verse. It does not matter if he knows or not. As you play the game, eventually he will pick up the tool that matches the verse.
Examples:

Sweep, sweep, sweep.
Make it neat.

Scrub, scrub, scrub.
Mop it clean.

Rake, rake, rake.
Make it neat.

Dig, dig, dig.
Dig it deep.

Encore

As your toddler learns to manipulate tools in correct ways, you will see a new sense-of-self emerging. By encouraging him to use tools in correct ways you are supporting his sense of self-accomplishment and giving him the joy that accompanies achievement. Supervise your toddler while he experiments with other interesting tools including:

◆ Flashlight   ◆ Magnifying glass
◆ Stamps and stamp pads   ◆ Scrub brush

It's the Same

Look, look, and you will see
The face in the mirror looks just like me.

Overture ....

How things are the same or different is a hard concept for toddlers to grasp. Verbalizing the differences between objects or naming the way they are the same will help your toddler understand *attributes*.

Performance ....

Play: To help your toddler learn how to match identical objects, play "It's the Same."

What you will need: Three pairs of toys such as: two books, two bears, two balls

How to play: Randomly place the pairs of toys on the floor between you and your toddler. Pick up one toy and ask, "Which one is like this one?" Then pick up the matching toy. Hold them both and say something like this: "They are the same. See? Two books." Then place them back on the floor. Repeat, picking up another toy and then the matching toy. Verbalize that they are the same. Next, have your toddler pick up one of the toys and you pick up the matching toy. An advanced version of the game is to pick up a toy and have your toddler pick up the one that is the same.

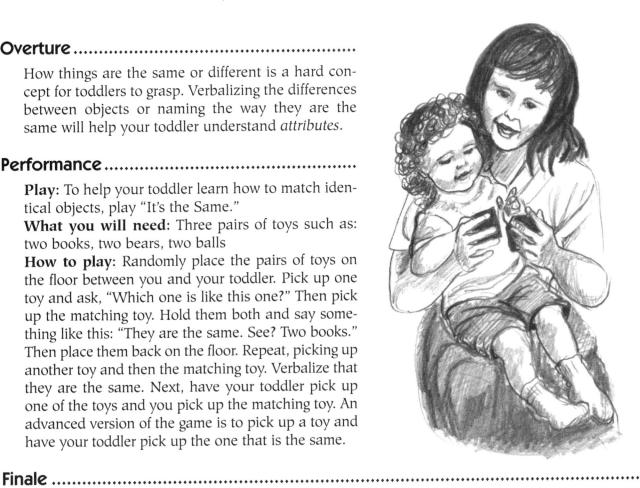

Finale ....

Use the rhyme and a plastic mirror to help your toddler learn that *same* means looking alike. Point to the toddler's image in the mirror and say something like: "You look like this." Look at your image and your toddler's image together in a mirror and say, "We do not look the same."

Encore ....

On other occasions, using pairs of objects, have your toddler match them. Objects should vary. Examples:
- ◆ Three different pairs of fruits: apples, oranges, and bananas
- ◆ Three different pairs of colored socks
- ◆ Three pairs of mittens with different designs
- ◆ Three different pairs of shoes of varied sizes
- ◆ Three pairs of plastic eating utensils: spoons, forks, and knives
- ◆ Three different pairs of seashells (pairs should be very similar to each other, but each set of shells should be different shapes)

It's Not the Same

Red, yellow, blue
Mittens, socks, and shoes.

Overture...

For the year-and-a-half-old child, distinguishing between things takes skill. Watch your toddler when he is given a choice. Sometime during the next six months he will begin to show a preference for certain colors, flavors, and textures.

Performance..

Play: To help your toddler distinguish between things that do not belong in a group of similar objects, play "It's Not the Same."

What you will need: Two apples, two bananas, two lemons, basket

How to play: Wash the fruit so it can be handled by your toddler. Seat your toddler on the floor. Place the basket of fruit on the floor between you and your toddler. Say something like this: "Which pieces of fruit are the same?" Your toddler may not understand the concept of *same*. Show your toddler the two apples. Place them side by side on the floor. Tell your toddler, "They are the same—apples." Then put a banana on the floor with the apples. Ask, "Which one is *not the same*;—which one is different?" Play with the fruits three at a time in this way until your toddler can pick out the fruit that does not belong in a group. Eat some of the fruit after the session. Let your toddler pick which one he wants for a snack.

Finale..

Use pairs of shoes, socks, or mittens to play the same sort of game. Place one pair and an unmatched mitten, shoe, or sock in a row. Ask your toddler to point out the one that is "different." On other occasions, verbalize which of the objects' attributes are different.
Example:
- ◆ The cat and dog are different because the cat is *little* and our dog is *big*.
- ◆ The soup and salad are different, because the soup is *hot* and the salad is *cold*.

Encore ....

As your toddler becomes familiar with the terms *same* and *different*, ask questions about the attributes (size, color, shape) of common familiar objects that he sees.
- ◆ Are these socks the same color? (Do they match?)
- ◆ Are these eggs the same shape?
- ◆ Are the kittens different colors?
- ◆ Which ball is a different shape?
- ◆ Are you and Daddy the same size?
- ◆ Are the apple and banana the same color/shape?

Keeping Track

Milestone	Date	Comments
Explores objects by shaking, banging, throwing, dropping		
Can find hidden objects		
Can imitate a facial expression		
Knows how to talk on the telephone		
Can recognize parts of the face		
Can recognize parts of the body		
Can recognize positions: "up," "down," "under," and "around"		
Enjoys hearing short stories		
Enjoys simple household chores		
Pretends to do adult work		
Uses non-toy materials with handles		
Can match identical objects		
Can distinguish unlike objects		

"Mine!"

Social/Emotional Development

Contemplate

One of a toddler's most difficult jobs is learning to separate from his parents. An eighteen-month-old is just learning that he is a separate individual—not part of his mother. He is still learning that he has his own body, desires, and a voice to express these desires. How a toddler expresses his separateness will vary. Some protest violently. Some throw tantrums. Others are aggressive. All of these ways of protesting are healthy ways to handle separation. When a toddler has a strong feeling about something, he needs to have that feeling validated by someone who will listen and talk to him.

Children this age have no social skills. When playing with other children they may bite, pull hair, scratch, or hit. Aggressive behavior is a toddler's way of testing the world. Overreacting to this kind of aggression gives it a great deal of significance. When a toddler is aggressive, it is an opportunity to teach him about other people's feelings. Say something like, "No one likes to be hit. When you hit your friend, he won't want to come back to play with you." Repeat these kinds of instructions over and over until the child abandons aggressive behavior. If a child is treated with aggression—spanked or hit—for being aggressive, his behavior is reinforced.

The only way a toddler can learn to socialize is by socializing. The more opportunities you give your toddler to be with peers, the more experiences he will have. The games and activities that are offered in this section will help your toddler practice appropriate social behavior.

Social/Emotional Milestones: 18 to 24 Months

- ◆ Will play in a mostly solitary rather than social way
  (will not understand cooperation or sharing yet)
- ◆ Will still relate better to adults than to other children
- ◆ Will begin to show increasing independence
- ◆ Will begin to engage in imitative play
- ◆ Will begin to imitate adult behavior
- ◆ Will express affection for family
- ◆ Will begin showing affection for peers
- ◆ Will begin to meet his own emotional needs by using a soft toy or doll
- ◆ Will learn to understand words that describe feelings (happy, sad, angry)
- ◆ Will begin to show his unique personality
- ◆ Will enjoy interactive games such as tag
- ◆ Will especially enjoy making things
- ◆ Will especially enjoy outings of all kinds

 **General Tips**

Toddlers learn a great deal from watching others. At times it will be almost comical to watch your toddler's hand gestures, facial expressions, and body language because it will be like looking into a mirror. Since toddlers are such "copycats" at this age, it is vital that they have an opportunity to be with peers. A play group or at least two or three regular friends is important for your toddler's social and emotional growth.

Toddlers need peers. Several regular playmates is enough, but a play group is even better. This is a critical time to get your child out into the world of other children. Playtime is the time to learn about relationships. Toddlers can learn about socialization from other children.

Although toddlers enjoy being with other children, they will not know how to be good playmates yet. One-and-a-half-year-olds do not know how to play cooperatively. Instead, they play parallel. Two toddlers will play side by side, but seldom interact or share a game. Not even acknowledging each other, they will pick up play habits with their peripheral vision. If you watch children this age playing together, you will seldom see them interacting, but they may play identical games.

The second year seems to highlight personality differences among toddlers. The quiet toddler may become more timid. The loud, boisterous toddler may become hyperactive. Children at this age have a full spectrum of abilities. Do not become concerned by these differences; see them as a natural growing process. It can be detrimental to your child's ability to relate to others if you see any part of her nature as "bad" or unacceptable. Embrace your toddler's uniqueness. Do not compare one toddler to another. Celebrate your toddler's quirks; support her struggles and triumphs.

Although it may seem that your toddler will be a baby forever, she will not. These days will come and go all too quickly. Take time to appreciate your toddler. The way you treat her today may well be the way she will treat herself for the rest of her life.

Social/Emotional Development 18- to 24-Month-Old

Share the Toy

Let us be kind to one another,
As brothers ought to be.

Overture

Watch your toddler closely, and you will see an expansion of moods, playing, thinking, talking, and socializing which all reflect underlying brain growth.

Performance

Play: To teach your toddler to begin playing in a cooperative way, play "Share the Toy."
What you will need: One toy
How to play: Sit on the floor with the toddler. Hand him the toy and let him hold it. Then say, "Will you share the toy?" Try to talk your toddler into letting you hold the toy for a few seconds. Talk about how nice it is that he is sharing with you. Then give the toy back. Take turns with the toy. This game may need to be played many times before your toddler will even begin to understand how to share something.

Finale

If the concept of sharing is too difficult for your toddler, play with two toys. Trade toys every so often. Interact with a game using the two toys. For example, play with a bucket and a shovel in the sandbox. Use the shovel to put sand in the toddler's bucket. Then give him the shovel and ask him to put sand in the bucket while you hold it. Limit the time to a few minutes when playing games of sharing. When an older child is visiting or playing with your toddler, try the one-toy-method of play. Play this sharing game for only a few minutes. At this age, introducing the concepts of sharing and cooperating is all that is needed. A toddler is not emotionally mature enough to be patient and cooperative for more than a few seconds or minutes. When your toddler is in a play situation with another toddler, provide two identical toys with which the toddlers may play.

Encore

Make words like "cooperation," "sharing," and "helping" part of your toddler's listening vocabulary. During the day, point out to your toddler how people work cooperatively.

- At the supermarket—Note that the boy bagging the groceries is helping the woman who is checking out your food.
- At the doctor's office—Explain that the nurse is helping the doctor.
- When watching sports—Tell your toddler that the team members are working together.
- When you see a police officer—Explain that he is helping keep people safe.
- When stopped at a stoplight—Explain that people cooperate by going through the intersection when the light is green and stopping when the light is red; they take turns.

Playmates

You shall learn to play with me and learn to use my toys;
And then I think that we shall be two happy little boys.

Overture

Watch your toddler playing with others, and you will see a great deal of learning taking place.

Performance

Play: To help your toddler relate to peers, provide time with playmates the same age.

What you will need: Play group or several other toddlers

How to play: Provide a time (30 to 45 minutes is long enough) several times each week for your toddler to play with peers. There should be no more than six in the group with two caregivers supervising. Provide a variety of toys in a safe, confined area. Set reasonable limits for the toddlers and maintain those limits consistently. Deal with difficult situations as they arise and before they get out of control. Sometimes, join the toddlers at play, but mostly give them time to play while observing from a distance.

Finale

If one child is aggressive to the others, talk to her about it. Explain that the other children do not like to be bitten, or slapped, or punched. Tell the toddler that it hurts the other child. Do not expect a toddler to share her very favorite toy. If your toddler has a "lovie," put it away during the play-group time. Provide identical toys for children who hate to share. Praise your toddler for playing in a group. On other occasions, take the toddler to a playground where she can observe children of various ages playing in a group. New playmates will provide opportunities for social stimulation that your toddler cannot get from adults at home.

Encore

An activity toddlers seem to be able to share is water play. Although it requires constant adult supervision, water play seems to be both interesting and versatile for toddlers. When weather permits, place a few inches (several centimeters) of water in a wading pool. If the weather is too cold for outside water games, put the toddler in a bathtub (only with adult surpervision) with several inches (several centimeters) of warm water. Provide plastic containers, measuring cups, buckets, shovels, etc. Water play soothes restlessness, dissipates tension, and heightens experimentation. Toddlers love to play with water in many ways:

- ◆ Use a hose and a bucket of warm water to wash large, plastic ride-on toys.
- ◆ Use a hose to water the grass, shrubs, or trees.
- ◆ Use a bucket of water to wash pebbles or rocks.
- ◆ Use a hose to help put water into a wading pool.
- ◆ Run through sprinklers.
- ◆ Use a hose, a bucket of warm water, and a scrub brush to wash the tires on the family car.
- ◆ Use a hose to squirt the porch or sidewalk.

Fly Away

Little Robin flew away. Where can little Robin be?
Gone into the cherry tree. Little Robin fly home to me.

Overture

Nerves that create emotions mature before the nerves that control emotions. Your toddler will not always know how to deal with the great emotions he is feeling. Discussing feelings and playing games that practice appropriate methods of handling negative feelings are good ways for your toddler to learn how to deal with emotional upsets.

Performance

Play: To encourage the toddler's independence and willingness to separate from an adult, play "Fly Away."

What you will need: No special equipment is needed to play this game.

How to play: Being separated from a parent is especially difficult for toddlers. Waving good-bye helps ease the pain of separation. You can give your toddler a special way of saying good-bye by teaching him how to blow a kiss. To assist your toddler in dealing with separation, play "Fly Away." Demonstrate how to flap your arms like wings and "fly away." Show the toddler how to throw a kiss. Then tell the toddler to "fly away." Then say, "Fly home." Take turns "flying" away and "flying" back into each other's arms.

Finale

Use the rhyme as signals for the "Fly Away" game.
Example:
   Little Robin fly away. (*Toddler flaps arms and runs away to hide.*)
   Where can little Robin be? (*Look around for the toddler.*)
   Gone into the cherry tree. (*Look at the toddler.*)
   Little Robin fly home to me. (*Toddler flaps arms and returns to adult's arms.*)
On other occasions, use a varied version of the rhyme to name the place the toddler is hiding.
Example:
   Little Robin fly away. (*Toddler flaps arms and hides.*)
   Where can little Robin be? (*Parent calls to the toddler.*)
   Gone behind the sofa. (*Name the place where the toddler is hiding.*)
   Little Robin fly home to me. (*Toddler flaps arms and returns to adult's arms.*)

Encore

Play a reverse version of hide-and-seek. Tell your toddler where to hide. Say something like this: "Go hide behind the sofa." While the toddler is hiding, close your eyes, count to ten, and then go to find him. Telling your toddler where to hide will develop his listening skills and help him learn to follow directions. Repeat the game suggesting a variety of places to hide.

Pizza Dough

Heigh O, heigh O, heigh O!
Can you see my pizza dough?

Overture

Your toddler's improved memory and problem-solving skills will make it possible for her to engage in make-believe play. Watch when she is playing alone, and you will see her engaging in pretend play.

Performance

Play: To encourage imitative play, pretend to knead and play with imaginary pizza dough.
What you will need: No special equipment is needed to play this game.
How to play: Pretend to have pizza dough in your hands. Pat and roll the big ball of dough. Show the toddler what you can do with the imaginary dough: roll it, stretch it, knead it, throw it up into the air and catch it. Pass the imaginary pizza dough to your toddler. Encourage her to pretend she is playing with pizza dough. Name things for her to do with the dough.

Finale

Use the rhyme to knead real pizza or bread dough. Frozen bread dough, thawed to room temperature can be kneaded by small hands. Give the toddler a small handful of dough to knead on a floured board. After she has played with the dough for awhile (do not be surprised if she does not want to give it back), put the kneaded dough into a buttered bowl and cover it. Let it rise as directed on the package. Punch it down, and then let your toddler knead it again. Place it in a buttered pan and repeat the rising step. Then bake the dough until the top is brown and crusty.
On other occasions, use various versions of the verse to mime.
Examples:
> Heigh O, heigh O, heigh O!
> Can you see me wearing a hat?
> (*Put on imaginary hat.*)

> Heigh O, heigh O, heigh O!
> Can you see me eating a lemon?
> (*Make sour faces.*)

> Heigh O, heigh O, heigh O!
> Can you see my hot potato?
> (*Pretend to pass something hot back and forth between your hands.*)

Encore

The more interesting things your toddler sees, the richer will be her fantasy world. After playing with dough, try to arrange for your toddler to visit:
- ◆ A pizza restaurant where the cooks throw the dough in the air
- ◆ A bakery where fresh bread is made
- ◆ A doughnut shop where doughnuts are made fresh each day

Rock-a-By, Dolly

Close your eyes, Dolly. Do not peek.
Rock-a-by, Dolly. Go to sleep.

Overture

Watching your toddler turn into a walking, talking, wonder-filled child is delightful. When you see your child pretending to be the mommy or daddy in play, you will realize just how important you are as a role model.

Performance

Play: To encourage your toddler to imitate nurturing behavior, play "Rock-a-By, Dolly."
What you will need: Child-sized rocking chair; small, realistic vinyl or rubber baby doll (without hair or moveable eyes); baby blanket; toy baby bottle
How to play: Wrap the doll in a baby blanket. Demonstrate how to use the toy baby bottle to "feed" the doll. Show your toddler how to rock the doll. Sit your toddler in the rocking chair. Hand him the doll. Take turns rocking and feeding the doll.

Finale

Use the rhyme to sing a lullaby while rocking the doll. Whisper the words. Sing the words. Say the words in a sing-song voice. Try a variety of easy-to-use ways to present the rhyme. See if your toddler tries to sing to Dolly. On other occasions, use a doll to get an unwilling toddler to do things he needs to do.

◆ If your toddler does not want to get ready for bed, first have him undress Dolly and get her ready for bed.
◆ If the toddler does not want to eat, pretend to let Dolly taste some of his food.
◆ If the toddler does not want to take a bath, first undress Dolly and put her in the bathtub.
◆ If your toddler does not want to get dressed, dress Dolly first.

Encore

Rocking is often very comforting for toddlers. Some toddlers rock themselves back and forth in their cribs. If your toddler seems to enjoy being rocked, spend time comforting him in this way. Too soon, it may seem, your baby will think he is too big to be rocked, and these days of rocking chairs and lullabies will be gone forever. Enjoy them while you can. Here is a lullaby that has been sung by mothers for over one hundred years:

Lulla, lulla, lullaby,
Softly sleep, my baby;
Lulla, lulla, lullaby,
Soft, soft, my baby.

Kiss Me Quick

Kiss me quick before I blink.
Kiss me quick before I wink.

Overture

Watch your toddler when she is around others, and you may discover that she is becoming quite affectionate. Encourage and praise your toddler for being affectionate, but do not force her to be affectionate to someone if she chooses not to be.

Performance

Play: To encourage your toddler to express affection for family members, play "Kiss Me Quick."
What you will need: No special equipment is needed to play this game.
How to play: Sit with your toddler in your lap. Demonstrate a blink with both eyes and a wink with one eye. Say "Blink" as you are blinking both eyes. Say "Wink" as you are winking with one eye. Then say, "Kiss me quick before I blink." Kiss your toddler before you blink. When you say "Kiss me quick," give your toddler the chance to kiss you before you blink or wink. (Do not expect that your toddler will be able to wink with one eye, but she will probably like blinking with both eyes.)

Finale

Use a slightly different version of the rhyme to incorporate other acts of affection: hug, squeeze, snuggle, hold, embrace, love, cradle, cuddle.
Examples:
> Hug me quick before I blink.
> Squeeze me quick before I wink.
>
> Snuggle me quick before I blink.
> Hold me quick before I wink.

Use the game with family members. Example: "Kiss Daddy before he winks." On other occasions, use "before you blink" and "before I wink" to reinforce the names of body parts. Say something like this, "Touch your toes before I blink."
Examples:
> Touch your nose before I blink.
> Wiggle your toes before I wink.
> Shake my hand before I blink.

Encore

Teach your toddler a variety of ways to give affection including:
- ◆ Blowing a kiss when saying good-bye
- ◆ Bear hugging (big hug and kiss like a big animal)
- ◆ Butterfly kissing (open and close eyelashes on another's cheek)
- ◆ Giving high-fives
- ◆ Shaking hands

Everybody Loves a Hug

I love you well, my little brother.
And you are fond of me.

Overture

Watch your toddler when he is around another child who is crying, and you will probably see just how affectionate he can be. If another child hurts himself, your toddler may rush to his rescue and offer a hug or other demonstration of affection.

Performance

Play: To encourage your toddler to show affection to peers, play "Everybody Loves a Hug."
What you will need: Doll, stuffed animal, teddy bear
How to play: Demonstrate the game "Everybody Loves a Hug" by hugging each of the toys. First say "Everybody loves a hug, even bears." Then hug the bear. Say, "Everybody loves a hug, even dolls." Then hug the doll. Repeat with other stuffed toys. Then say, "Everybody loves a hug, even (toddler's name). Hug your toddler. Then say the line and hand your toddler the appropriate toy to hug. Later when he knows the game better, let the toddler pick up and hug the toys as you mention each one.

Finale

Use the rhyme to encourage your toddler to hug his siblings (substituting "sister" for "brother" when appropriate. Or replace "brother" with "father," "uncle," "grandma," etc. Follow the rhyme with hugs between your toddler and the family member. On other occasions, when your toddler is sad, bored, lonely, sick, or tired tell him, "You look like you could use a hug." And give him a big hug. When you need a hug, ask your toddler for it. Say something like: "I sure could use a hug." Let your toddler know how much you enjoy his hugs. Toddlers cannot do many things to help grownups, but the love they give is tremendous. It will make your toddler feel very important when he knows you need and want his affection.

Encore

Hugs can become as reinforcing as verbal praise. Hugs are the silent way to say, "You are extraordinary, and I am proud of you." For several months, each time you hug your child, say something especially encouraging. After a while, the hug will trigger the same feelings as the verbal praise. Many physical games that you play with your toddler can end with a hug.

- ◆ Hide-and-seek—when you find your toddler, give him a big hug.
- ◆ Tag—when you catch your toddler, give him a hug.
- ◆ Wrestling—when you are wrestling with your toddler, give him a bear hug.

Which Is Your Favorite One?

Pick 'em, pick 'em, pick just one.
Which is your favorite one?

Overture..

Watch your toddler when you offer a treat that she likes, and she probably will not hesitate before making her choice. The more opportunities you give your toddler to choose, the better choices she will be able to make.

Performance..

Play: To encourage your toddler to use a soft toy or doll as a special "lovie," play "Which Is Your Favorite One?"

What you will need: A variety of toddler's favorite soft toys

How to play: Line up five or six toys, and tell your toddler to pick one. Then talk about her choice. Then line them all up in a different order and ask your toddler to pick one. Then talk about that toy. Keep rearranging and letting the toddler pick one. Repeat this game with a variety of toys for a series of days. What seems to be your toddler's favorite soft toy? Tuck the one you think might be her favorite in bed with her each night. Using a soft toy for security will help your toddler sleep through the night. A drop of your perfume on the "lovie" will make it feel even more familiar, comforting, and special to your toddler.

Finale ....

Use the rhyme to encourage your toddler to make choices about other things. When giving her a snack, line up two or three choices and recite the rhyme. When toddlers are given many choices, they learn to make wise decisions, and it gives them a good feeling of having power.

Encore ....

On other occasions, use the rhyme to give the toddler choices.

Examples:

- ◆ When choosing a vegetable for dinner, show the toddler the cans/packages with pictures of corn, peas, or another vegetable. Recite the rhyme and let your toddler choose.
- ◆ When cutting up fruit for your toddler's snack, line up a banana, apple, and orange. Recite the rhyme and let your toddler choose.
- ◆ When dressing your toddler, set out two or three outfits. Recite the rhyme and let your toddler choose what she will wear that day.

If You're Happy

If you're happy and you know it, clap your hands.
If you're happy and you know it, clap your hands.
If you're happy and you know it, and you really want to show it,
If you're happy and you know it, clap your hands.
—Traditional Song

Overture

Watch your toddler at play, and you will see his natural rhythm at work. Movement activities will help your toddler learn with his whole body.

Performance

Play: To help your toddler learn to recognize and express joy, play "If You're Happy."
What you will need: No special equipment is needed to play this game.
How to play: Take advantage of your toddler's desire to learn language, especially the names for parts of his own body. To play the game, touch a part of toddler's body and name it—"leg." Say it again and again, each time touching that body part. Then touch another part of his body and name it. Begin with just a few parts and add new ones when you play the game on other days.

Finale

Use the song to celebrate the parts of the body that your toddler can name. Sing the song with a variety of verses. Touch a body part and then sing a verse. Pause when it is time to name the body part, giving your toddler a chance to say the word.
Examples:

> If you're happy and you know it, touch your (pause) toes. (*Repeat.*)
> If you're happy and you know it, and you really want to show it,
> If you're happy and you know it, touch your (pause) toes.

> If you're happy and you know it, slap your (pause) legs. (*Repeat.*)
> If you're happy and you know it, and you really want to show it,
> If you're happy and you know it, slap your (pause) legs.

On other occasions, play a guessing game. Touch a body part and ask, "Is this your leg? No, this is not your leg. This is your arm." Ask questions and see if your toddler can nod or shake his head accordingly.

Encore

Use the same game to express other feelings such as "mad" and "sad" in appropriate ways.
Examples:

> If you're mad and you know it, stomp your feet. (*Repeat.*)
> If you're mad and you know it, and you really want to show it,
> If you're mad and you know it, stomp your feet.

> If you're sad and you know it, hug yourself. (*Repeat.*)
> If you're sad and you know it, and you really want to show it,
> If you're sad and you know it, hug yourself.

Look! It's You!

Polly, Dolly, Kate, and Molly,
All are filled with pride and folly.
Polly tattles, dolly wriggles,
Katy rattles, Molly giggles. . . .
—Traditional Rhyme

Overture

Watch your toddler, and you will see her uniqueness coming to life. During the second year, children begin to develop distinctive personalities.

Performance

Play: To acknowledge your toddler's uniqueness, play "Look! It's You!"
What you will need: Plastic hand mirror
How to play: Place the toddler on your lap, facing the hand mirror. Hold it in front of the toddler so she can gaze into it and see her own face. Talk about your toddler's physical characteristics.
Examples:
- You have big blue eyes. See your beautiful blue eyes.
- You have soft red hair. Look at your pretty hair.
- You have beautiful black skin. See your wonderful skin.

Finale

When your toddler exhibits her unique personality characteristics, praise each one. Accepting your toddler's basic nature will give her permission to be exactly who she is. Your acceptance is a message of unconditional love.
- You are very quiet like a little mouse. Quiet is good.
- You like to move around a lot. Active is great.
- You do not like it when I leave you. It makes you cry. It makes me sad when I cannot be with you, too. However, I will always return to you.

When your toddler is present, share her uniqueness with others.
- (Toddler's name) is quiet as a mouse. Isn't that nice?
- (Toddler's name) likes to move. Watch her leap about the area.
- (Toddler's name) is gentle with the kitty. See how gentle and kind she is.

Encore

Your toddler will begin to feel a variety of feelings. Let your child know that all of her feelings are okay and that having feelings is part of the human experience. Reassure her when she is anxious.
- If you are shopping and your toddler begins to cry. Instead of telling her to "be good," explain that you understand that she is tired. Say, "I know that you are tired of shopping. You want to go home and rest. I will take you home so you can have your nap now."
- If your child is afraid to go into her room when it is dark, you might say something like this: "I will turn on this night-light so you can see that you are safe. Remember, I am nearby, and I will keep you safe."
- If your child is jealous of a sibling you might say: "I can understand how sometimes you may feel jealous of the attention I give others, but I can love more than one person. I will always love you, too."

Tag

Tag! You're It!

Overture

Toddlers are enthusiastic and energetic, but they need constant supervision. Finding constructive ways to help your toddler expend his high-level of energy will be important to his health and safety.

Performance

Play: To teach your toddler how to play an active, interactive game, play "Tag."

What you will need: No special equipment is needed to play tag.

How to play: Demonstrate how to tag your toddler and then run away. Say, "Tag, you're It." Teach the toddler how to chase you. When your toddler touches you, then reverse roles and you chase your toddler. Although the rules for tag are simple ones, it may take time for your toddler to understand when to chase and when to run away. Do not be surprised if your toddler switches roles for no apparent reason.

Finale

Play tag when you have a small group of children together. Even a group of older siblings will make good sports for games of tag. The more opportunity your toddler has to play in interactive games, the more quickly he will learn social skills needed for preschool and school. On other occasions, when trying to distract your toddler, a game of tag might get his mind off something else. For example, if your toddler does not want to leave the park, a game of tag may bring him closer to the car. Or if your toddler does not really want to get into the bathtub, a game of tag can entice him into the bathroom.

Encore

Now that your toddler has developed the strength and coordination for running games, he has also developed the mental ability to understand imaginative twists to physical games. Play imaginary running games. Some game ideas include:

◆ Let's run to the jungle and find a monkey.
◆ Let's run up a mountain into the clouds.
◆ Let's run along the beach at sunset.
◆ Let's run like the wind.
◆ Lets run in the snow and throw snowballs.
◆ Let's swim underwater and see all the fish.
◆ Let's run like we are deer.
◆ Let's run up this steep, steep hill. Then we'll run back down again.

Be My Valentine

Roses are red. Violets are blue.
Sugar is sweet, and so are you.
—Traditional Rhyme

Overture

Watch your toddler when she is using crayons. Toddlers will often draw on any surface—tables, walls, clothes, face, and hands. When using crayons, a one-and-a-half-year-old has to be very closely supervised. In the beginning, crayons might be a toy you will want to keep hidden except when being used.

Performance

Play: To give your toddler the joy of creating something beautiful, make valentines. It does not have to be February 14 to exchange messages of love.

What you will need: Red and pink construction paper, scissors, geometric-shaped paper cutouts, glue stick or stickers, crayons

How to play: Cut large heart-shapes from red and pink construction paper. Using a glue stick, show your toddler how to attach paper cutouts or stickers to the valentine. When the glue dries, scribble on the valentine with crayons. Let your toddler make several. Hang them all around the room. Write the date on the back of her first valentine, and put it away in a safe place so you can give it to her when she is older.

Finale

Write the rhyme on a valentine that you make for your child. Recite the verse while you are creating valentines. Replace the word "sugar" in the verse with your child's name and personalize the last line.

Example:
> Roses are red.
> Violets are blue.
> (Toddler's name) is sweet,
> and Daddy is, too.

Encore

On other occasions, recite personalized versions of the rhyme, depending on the occasion.

Examples:
- Roses are red. Violets are blue. I am hungry, are you, too?
- Roses are red. Violets are blue. You hug me and I'll hug you.
- Roses are red. Violets are blue. Put on your socks and shoes, too.
- Roses are red. Violets are blue. You are terrific. I love you!

An Outing Today, Hurrah!

Where have you been all the day, my boy, Willy?
Where have you been all the day, my boy, Willy? . . .
—Traditional Rhyme

Overture

Among the earliest experiences that influence the development of a child's view of himself are those with other people, especially with the significant people in his life: parents, siblings, and peers. If the child is accepted, respected, and liked for what he is, he will be helped immeasurably toward a healthy attitude of respect for himself.

Performance

Play: Plan weekly or monthly outings.
What you will need: Transportation
How to play: Outings stimulate and inspire a toddler's social and emotional growth. At least once a month, set aside a day to take your toddler somewhere interesting. When you are out, do not be in a hurry. Talk about what your toddler sees, hears, tastes, touches, and smells. Take time to enjoy all aspects of the journey. Vary your trips to include:

- ◆ Park
- ◆ Playground
- ◆ Zoo
- ◆ Museum
- ◆ Aquarium
- ◆ Circus
- ◆ Amusement park
- ◆ Public library

Finale

Use the rhyme after an outing, and then talk about where you have been. Ask the question "Where have we been?" Then verbalize points of interest. Example: "We went to the park today. We rode on the merry-go-round. We fed the ducks in the pond. Wasn't it fun at the park today?"

Encore

Toddlers use their eyes, ears, hands, noses, and mouths to experience new things. It is good to experience the world with all of these extraordinary senses. Outings are a perfect way to provide multiple sensory experiences that stimulate growth and learning. For several days after each outing, reminisce about your experiences to recall how the five senses were stimulated during the outing. Example:

- ◆ When we went to the park, we ate ice cream cones.
- ◆ When we went to the zoo, we heard the parrots.
- ◆ When we went to the circus, we saw the monkeys dance.

Find a Happy Face

Overture ....

Toddlers do not usually understand the language of feelings. Although they have feelings—sometimes frustrating ones because they cannot communicate their needs and desires to others—they cannot articulate them. Studying pictures of people expressing emotion on their faces is a good way to introduce the language of feelings.

Performance ....

Play: To introduce your toddler to the idea that people wear feelings on your faces, play "Find a Happy Face."

What you will need: Magazines with pictures of people

How to play: Holding your toddler in your lap so she can see the pictures, turn the pages of the magazine and point out happy faces. Then ask your child to "find a happy face" on each page.

Finale ....

When your child understands the correlation between smiling and happiness, one at a time, introduce other feelings by finding faces in magazines that express them. Begin with the most basic ones such as anger, sadness, worry, etc. Later, using a mirror, have your toddler make faces to express happiness, sadness, anger.

Encore ....

When reading stories to your toddler, make note of the faces of the characters and ask questions such as:

- Do the three pigs look worried in this picture?
- Does Papa bear look angry in this picture?
- Does Cinderella look sad in this picture?
- Who looks the happiest in this picture?

Keeping Track

Milestone	Date	Comments
Working toward cooperation and sharing		
Relates best to adults/ can relate to children		
Beginning to show independence		
Engages in imitative play		
Imitates adult behavior		
Expresses affection for family		
Shows affection for peers		
Meets own emotional needs/doll		
Enjoys hearing stories		
Shows a unique personality		
Enjoys interactive games/tag		
Enjoy crafts		
Enjoys outings		

PLAYING

With Your Toddler

24- to 36-Months Old

I'll Do It Myself!

Fine Motor Development

Contemplate

Often adults interpret a two-year-old's desire to become independent as defiant behavior. Do not take it personally if your toddler no longer wants your help doing all the things you are used to doing for him. When a toddler wants to do something that an adult can do better and more quickly, it is hard to be patient. Although it is tedious to sit and watch your toddler struggling, it is important that you do just that. Pat yourself on the back every time you let your youngster do something by himself. Instead of jumping in and doing things for him, be patient and encourage him to do things on his own. He will develop more autonomy each time you support his exploration. In his struggle to become independent, he will have many opportunities to develop fine motor and gross motor skills.

Giving your toddler the space he needs to care for himself is a way of demonstrating your confidence in him, and it will empower him. Two-year-olds gain many fine motor skills during the third year of development. Below are a list of just a few. However, keep in mind that children develop at different rates; do not be alarmed if by his third birthday your toddler has not mastered all of the milestones listed. This chapter on fine motor skills offers fun-filled activities to introduce and reinforce each milestone listed below.

Fine Motor Milestones: 24 to 36 Months

◆ Will begin to hold a pencil in the correct position for writing
◆ Will learn to draw vertical and horizontal lines and circular strokes
◆ Will learn to build towers with four or more blocks
◆ Will learn how to turn a rotating handle to open a door
◆ Will learn how to push to close a door
◆ Will learn how to screw and unscrew lids
◆ Will learn how to take off and put on his own socks
◆ Will learn how to take off his own shoes
◆ Will learn how to unbutton large buttons
◆ Will learn how to use a pincher grip to pick up small objects
◆ Will learn to turn pages of a book or magazine one at a time
◆ Will learn to drink from a cup and eat with a spoon
◆ Will learn how to put things into a container and take them out again
◆ Will learn to put toys in a box or container

 General Tips

Watch a toddler concentrating on a task, and you will see learning taking place. It is delightful to watch a two-year-old gathering information through play. *Playing is a toddler's work.* The way youngsters discover how things work brings them great pleasure and gives them practice with fine motor skills.

Demonstrating to your toddler how a particular toy or object works will limit its uses. If left alone to explore, your toddler will find dozens of ways to play with something as simple as a measuring cup or cardboard box. Do not stifle creativity or limit your toddler's rich fantasy world by imposing rules and regulations on her play. *Praise creativity and imagination* as well as her ability to master new skills.

It is important to remember: a two-year-old does not learn how to do something after only one lesson. There are many levels of learning. Slowly and carefully work on one level of learning until it is mastered; then move to the next level. One way to teach your toddler how to do something is to take her through four simple steps:

- ◆ Have her watch you do it.
- ◆ Have her help you do it.
- ◆ Help her do it.
- ◆ Watch her do it.

When teaching a toddler to do something, remember, praise is a powerful teaching tool. Never redo something that your toddler has worked hard to do.

Appropriate toys and tools for a toddler include:

- ◆ Puzzles with giant pieces
- ◆ Wooden blocks to stack
- ◆ Large crayons and paper for supervised play
- ◆ A soft hairbrush for brushing hair
- ◆ A small soft toothbrush
- ◆ Plastic cup, spoon, and other toy dishes
- ◆ Toys on wheels with a handle for pulling
- ◆ A play telephone
- ◆ Balls to roll and throw
- ◆ Child-sized table or desk where she can work
- ◆ Soft toy for comfort—especially a teddy bear
- ◆ Music box or musical toy
- ◆ Dolls

My Book

This is my book; take a look.
This is my book; it's full of my work.

Overture

Scribbling is a very strong impulse and vital to a toddler's learning. You can help your toddler meet his need to scribble by providing large sheets of paper such as shelf paper or butcher paper and fat crayons. Supervise his scribbling sessions so he does not write on walls or furniture or chew on the crayons. Applaud every "work of art."

Performance

Play: To help your toddler learn how to hold a pencil in the correct position for writing, have the toddler "write" his own book.

What you will need: Large, spiral-bound drawing pad; primary pencil; place to sit and work

How to play: Encouraging your toddler to "write" his own book will make books seem more personal. It will give your toddler practice using a pencil, and when the book is completed, it will give you a great treasure. Place a large photograph of your toddler on the cover or first page of the drawing pad. Write his name in large letters under the photograph. Show the book to your toddler. Explain that the book is for him to write in. Tell him, "We do not write in all books, but this is a special book in which it is okay to write." Then give the toddler a primary pencil. (When your toddler is using a pencil, make sure he is sitting down and not walking around while holding the pencil.) A small child-sized desk or a high-chair tray makes a good work surface. Open to the first page in the book and let your toddler scribble. Work on "writing" the book for a little bit each day. Your toddler will create pages in random order and may sometimes work on a page for several days. Praise every effort your toddler makes when scribbling in his book. If he wants to use crayons and paints in his book—all the better!

Finale

Use the rhyme when you and your toddler look at the work in the book. Sit with your toddler in your lap so he can see his book. Recite the rhyme. Then turn each page and talk about how much you like looking at his scribbles. Do not identify anything the toddler draws as a specific object. Do not make comments such as: "This looks like a horse." or "Is this a cloud?" Instead, make comments such as: "I like the energy you have when you draw." Or say, "These lines are so beautiful, I love to look at your work." Never show your toddler how to draw a certain shape or object. Let the toddler tell you about his drawings.

Encore

Show the book to friends and family. Ask permission to share the book before you do so. Take great pride in your toddler's efforts and abilities. When you treasure his work, you are sending him a clear message of how much you value him as an individual.

Tracing and Erasing

Up and down, circle round.
Up and down, all around town.

Overture

Watch your toddler begin to draw. She will not start out with a planned idea of what she will draw. Toddlers usually scribble and then identify their work.

Performance

Play: To introduce and reinforce drawing vertical, horizontal, and circular strokes, play "Tracing and Erasing."

What you will need: Small chalkboard, chalk, wet sponge

How to play: Draw a straight vertical line on the chalkboard. Moisten your index finger on the wet sponge and erase the line by tracing it with your finger. Draw another straight vertical line. Wet your toddler's index finger with the sponge and let her use the wet finger to trace the vertical line. During the first session, just draw straight vertical lines for her to erase. Encourage the toddler to trace and erase the line with one stroke of an index finger. If she wants to scribble and not erase lines with a wet index finger, wait to try this activity again in a month or two. Once your toddler learns to erase a straight vertical line on the chalkboard, advance to horizontal lines. Eventually, draw small circles to trace and erase. Do not bore your child with this activity or spend too much time with it if she becomes disinterested.

Finale

Recite the rhyme while your toddler uses soap to draw lines on a tile wall while bathing. Special bathtub soap paint is also good for drawing and tracing lines and circles while in the tub. Lines and circles can also be drawn on steamed-up plastic mirrors.
Example:

    Up and down, (*Use your finger to draw a vertical line on a steamed-up mirror.*)
    Circle round. (*Use your finger to draw a circle on mirror, too.*)
    Up and down, (*Use your hand in an up-and-down movement to erase the line.*)
    All around town. (*Use your hand in a circular movement to erase the circle.*)

Chalk and mediums that can be drawn and then erased will give your child the freedom to experiment with shapes. Other mediums to use for drawing lines and circles on tile, plastic mirrors, or sidewalks include:

◆ Shaving cream   ◆ Whipped cream
◆ Mud   ◆ Instant pudding

Encore

Cut 1" x 4" (25 x 102 mm) strips of very fine sandpaper. Glue each one horizontally or vertically on 5" by 8" (127 x 203 mm) index cards. Also, cut sandpaper into doughnut-shaped pieces and attach to index cards. Show your toddler how to trace the sandpaper lines and circles with her index finger.

Humpty Dumpty

Humpty Dumpty sat on a wall,
Humpty Dumpty had a great fall.
All the king's horses and all the king's men
Couldn't put Humpty Dumpty together again.
—Traditional Rhyme

Overture

Watch your toddler building block towers and knocking them down, and you may notice that his delight is in the knocking down—not the building up. The older he gets, the more important it will be to create constructions. Right now, the powerful feeling he gets from being able to make things topple will make playing with blocks one of his favorite games.

Performance

Play: To encourage the toddler to build taller and taller block towers, play "Humpty Dumpty."

What you will need: Wooden blocks, large plastic egg

How to play: Demonstrate how to build block walls three or four blocks high. Place the egg (Humpty Dumpty) on top of the wall. Recite the rhyme and let your toddler knock the wall down to give Humpty Dumpty a great fall.

Finale

During the third year, your toddler will learn to build towers four or more blocks high. Depending on the size of the blocks, his block constructions will become more detailed and sturdy. Introduce wooden linking toys and plastic linking blocks. Play construction with your toddler but always let him lead the play. If he wants to build things to topple down, play that game. If he wants to build towers and leave them standing to admire, let the toys remain where they are until he is ready to tear down the construction. Praise your child's buildings and have family members view and comment on them, too.

Encore

On other occasions, use wet sand or mud to build. To a toddler, sand and mud are special, magical substances. Most toddlers like to run their fingers through dry sand and squish mud between their toes. Mud and wet sand can be molded, pounded, rolled, squashed down flat, and left to dry and harden. Outside, in good weather, a small plastic wadding pool is a great place to make a wet sand-pile or a spot for making mud pies. Show the toddler how to use wet sand or mud in molds, such as plastic glasses to make castle walls, towers, and skyscrapers. A pile of garden soil or several bags of sand, a bucket of water, and old pie pans and plastic dishes will keep your toddler happy for hours on end.

Knock, Knock

Knock. Knock. Peek in.
Lift the latch. Walk in.

Overture

Watch your toddler playing with mechanical toys. During this third year, you will see her skills advance from awkward fumbling to the skillful working of intricate dials and switches. As your toddler gains fine motor skills, she will have an intense burst of interest in making things "work." As she masters each mechanical toy, she will lose interest in it and set it aside for something more challenging.

Performance

Play: To help your toddler learn how to turn a rotating handle like a doorknob, play "Knock, Knock."

What you will need: Door with a knob that turns

How to play: If the toddler does not already know how to open a door with a knob, demonstrate how to turn the doorknob. Turning a knob and pushing the door open at the same time requires coordination. If opening a door with a knob is too difficult for your toddler, just have her focus on turning the knob. Go to the other side of a closed door. Knock on the door and say, "Knock, knock." Ask, "Who is it?" Then say something like, "It is Mommy; may I come in?" Encourage your toddler to turn the knob and let you in. (You may have to push the door as she turns the knob.) Reverse positions and have your toddler knock on the door and say, "Knock, knock." Ask, "Who is it?" When she indicates who she is, let her into the room. Make believe your toddler is a welcomed guest who has just surprised you with a visit. "Oh, (toddler's name), I am so glad you came to see me! Please come in. I have been wanting to see you. I am so glad you are here at last!" Play at the door, opening and closing, until your toddler tires of the game.

Finale

Teach your toddler that when someone knocks on the door to the outside she is never to open the door. Explain that people do not just open the door without finding out first who is knocking. Demonstrate how to use the peephole or a window to look and find out who is at the door before opening it.

Encore

As your toddler learns how to manipulate knobs and handles, caution her about turning on hot water faucets. Take time to teach her how to turn small handles like water faucets and pull down on handles for flushing the toilet. Show your toddler which faucet is hot and which faucet is cold. Teach your toddler that the faucets should NEVER be touched while she is in the bathtub. Caution: To avoid scalding, turn down the hot water temperature as soon as your toddler learns how to turn on faucets. Adjust it so that water from a faucet at the very hottest setting will not burn her.

Fine Motor Development 24- to 36-Month-Old

Shut the Door

Shut the window,
Shut the door.

Overture

Watch your toddler pushing and pulling, and you will see him testing his strength. A more intense kind of exploration occurs when the two-year-old realizes he can make big, heavy things move in the direction he chooses.

Performance

Play: To practice pushing to close a door, play "Shut the Door."
What you will need: An inside door that is easy to push open and closed, oven mitt
How to play: Teaching your toddler how to close a door without also closing his fingers in the door is important. Demonstrate how to push on a door and close it with your palms flat against it. Explain that if fingers are wrapped around the edge of the door when it is shutting, they will get hurt. Put an oven mitt in the crack of a door and close it. Show the toddler how the oven mitt is squashed by the pressure of the door. Explain that fingers can be squashed in just that way when closed in a door. Open and close the door by pushing on it with the palm of your hand. Watch your toddler open and close the door by pushing with the palm of his hand. Practice.

Finale

Teach your toddler how to push a dresser drawer and a kitchen cupboard closed with palms flat on the surfaces. Explain that as with the door, fingers curved around the edge of a drawer or cupboard door will get pinched when it is shut. Practice pushing drawers and cupboard doors closed with palms flat on the surfaces. On other occasions, open and close doors while holding onto the door-knob or handle.

Encore

The outdoors represents a new and exciting environment for experimentation. Stores offer many new experiences for toddlers. Although stimulating, shopping can be a dangerous activity for two-year-olds. When shopping in stores, take time to explain the dangers including:
   ◆ Automatic opening doors—Standing on the wrong side of an automatic opening door can be dangerous. Stand on the inside of an automatic door and watch it fly open. Explain to your toddler that he is never to stand in front of the inside of doors in shopping malls and super-markets.
   ◆ Escalators—Riding on a fast moving escalator should be carefully supervised. Teach your toddler never to get on his hands and knees or put his fingers on the moving stairs. Teach him to stand, hold the side rail, and not walk while the escalator is in motion. (Be sure the child's shoelaces or clothing will not be caught in the escalator.)
   ◆ Crowds—Caution children about getting excited in large groups of shoppers. Explain that your child is not to visit with or leave a store with a stranger. Carefully explain what your toddler should do if he becomes separated from you and is lost in a crowd.

Marshmallows!

As soft as silk, light and puffy,
White as milk, sweet and fluffy.

Overture

Watch a toddler who is trying to unscrew a lid to get something she wants from inside a jar, and you will see just how quickly she can learn.

Performance

Play: To introduce and reinforce learning how to screw on and unscrew jar lids, play with miniature marshmallows. Picking up miniature marshmallows is also good for developing the pincher grip.

What you will need: Miniature marshmallows, four baby food jars with lids

How to play: Put a single marshmallow in one jar and screw on the lid. Fill one jar half-full of marshmallows, one jar full of marshmallows, and leave one jar empty. Screw on the lids. Show your toddler the four jars. Say something like this: "Let's put marshmallows in the empty jar." Demonstrate how to unscrew the lid of one jar to get the marshmallows. Have a conversation about the marshmallows that will motivate your toddler to unscrew the lids and redistribute the marshmallows.

Examples:
- ◆ Let's fill this jar full of marshmallows.
- ◆ Let's put more marshmallows in this jar.
- ◆ Let's take out all but one of the marshmallows in this jar.
- ◆ Let's put only one marshmallow in each of these two jars.

Allow the toddler free play time for manipulating marshmallows and jar lids. For safety reasons, do not give her the glass jars.

Finale

Use miniature marshmallows and regular-sized marshmallows for all sorts of games including:
- ◆ Indoor "snowball" fights
- ◆ Construction using marshmallows to connect blunt-ended toothpicks
- ◆ Sorting by size
- ◆ Make sugar plums by dipping miniature marshmallows into a bowl of milk and then into flavored gelatin powder.
- ◆ Make microwave treats. Put a chocolate bar and miniature marshmallows between two graham cracker squares and cook on high about 15-20 seconds. Cool before eating.

Encore

Use the rhyme as a riddle. Ask, "What is soft as silk, light and puffy, white as milk, and sweet and fluffy? (marshmallows) Use other food riddles as a guessing game. Provide several foods from which your toddler may choose to answer your food riddle.

Examples:
- ◆ What is red and round? (apple, banana, or orange?)
- ◆ What is cold and sweet? (ice cream, popcorn, or French fries?)

One Sock On

Deedle, deedle, dumpling, my son John,
Went to bed with his stockings on.
One shoe off, and one shoe on,
Deedle, deedle, dumpling, my son John.
　　　　　　　　　　—Traditional Rhyme

Overture

Once your toddler learns to dress and undress himself, a new independence will emerge. Some toddlers like to take off their clothing during the day. As soon as your toddler can take off his shoes and socks, do not be surprised if he does so at the most inopportune times.

Performance

Play: To help your toddler learn how to take off and put on socks, play "One Sock On."

What you will need: Three different colored pairs of your toddler's socks

How to play: Take off your toddler's shoes and socks. Lay the six socks in random order on the floor between you and your toddler. Put one sock on your toddler and say, "One sock on. One sock off." Assist your toddler in putting on the matching sock. Then instruct the toddler to take off one sock. Say, "One sock on. One sock off." Remove the other sock and replace it with a different colored sock on that foot. Say, "One sock on. One sock off." Repeat, matching, putting on, and taking off the socks.

Finale

Use a personalized version of the rhyme with the toddler's name to practice putting on and taking off socks. Begin by doing everything and eventually let your toddler put his socks on while you recite the rhyme.

Example:

　　Deedle, deedle, dumpling, (toddler's name) bear toes, (*Hold the feet in your hands.*)
　　Went to bed with his stockings off. (*Put on one sock.*)
　　One sock off, and one sock on, (*Put on the other sock.*)
　　Deedle, deedle, dumpling, my boy (toddler's name). (*Hold stockinged feet in your hands.*)

On other occasions, use the rhyme when putting on or taking off your toddler's shoes and socks, or recite it while he puts on or takes off his socks.

Encore

Letting your toddler choose what he will wear is a great opportunity for him to begin his independence. During this third year, your child will begin to show preferences for certain colors and styles. He will have favorite clothes that he likes to wear. Even if what he chooses to wear does not "match," is not appropriate for the occasion, or is not what you would like to see him wear, letting your toddler make these kinds of decisions will help him to become an able, self-caring person.

Shoe Store

One, two, buckle my shoe.
Three, four, shut the door. . . .
—Traditional Rhyme

Overture

For toddlers, the ritual of buying shoes in a shoe store is a great occasion. From the measuring of her foot, to the boxes of shoes the salesperson brings for her to try on, to parading around and looking in the on-the-floor mirrors, buying shoes usually holds a great deal of excitement for toddlers.

Performance

Play: To help your toddler learn how to take off and put on shoes, play "Shoe Store."
What you will need: Several pairs of your toddler's shoes (three or four pairs if possible), play money, mirror
How to play: Tell the toddler you are going to play shoe store. Invite her to pick a pair of shoes. Pretend to be a shoe salesperson and help your toddler try on the shoes. Tell her to try walking in them. Have her look at her feet in a mirror. Ask, "How do they feel?" If your toddler wants to "buy" the shoes, have her give you some play money. Then help your toddler take off the shoes and choose a different pair. As you play the game, have your toddler do more to put on and take off the shoes herself. Use pairs of adult-sized shoes to play the game in reverse. Let your toddler pretend to be the salesperson. You choose a pair of shoes, and have the toddler help you try on the shoes. Use play money to pay for the pairs of shoes you choose to buy.

Finale

Use a variety of shoes to have your toddler play a matching game. Place the shoes in a large basket, and have your toddler place pairs of shoes side by side in a "shoe parade."

Encore

Playing shoe store is a great way for toddlers to make choices, practice placing things in a basket or bags, and exchange play money. Other stores that you can set up to play with the toddler include:
- ◆ Fruit stand—Wash a variety of fruits and provide a basket for carrying selected fruits.
- ◆ Supermarket—Empty food boxes of various sizes and shapes make this game interesting and educational.
- ◆ Toy store—Toys, neatly lined up, will provide an interesting game of choosing for your toddler.
- ◆ Fast-food restaurant—Place pictures of fast foods, toy dishes, a small tray, Styrofoam containers, paper cups with straws, etc., on a shelf. Provide a small table where the pretend food can be "consumed."
- ◆ Clothing store—Some of your toddler's favorite outfits, folded and placed on a table or shelf, will provide a good shopping opportunity.
- ◆ Hardware store—Provide small tools from which your toddler can choose.

Button, Button

Button, button, who's got the button?

Overture..

Whether your toddler is more proficient at dressing or undressing, he will make a great deal of progress in self-care during his third year.

Performance..

Play: To help your toddler learn how to unbutton large buttons, play "Button, Button."
What you will need: A blouse, shirt, or jacket with large buttons
How to play: Put on the blouse, shirt, or jacket and button it up. Place your toddler in your lap facing you, then follow these four stages of instruction:

◆ Demonstrate how to unbutton the buttons without assistance from your toddler.
◆ Guide your child's hands in unbuttoning while doing most of it yourself.
◆ Help the child unbutton but do little of it yourself.
◆ Allow the child to unbutton the clothing alone, without your assistance.

Finale..

Use the rhyme to play the game "Button, Button, Who's Got the Button?" Put a large button in one hand. Right in front of your toddler, shift the button from one hand to the next. Back and forth. Not too fast. Then stop. Close both hands and extend them toward the toddler. Ask, "Button, button, who's got the button?" Ask your toddler to point to the hand with the button. Open that hand to show the button, then open the other hand if needed. Repeat. Play this game anytime you want to entertain your toddler: riding in a car or on a bus, while waiting in a supermarket line, etc. On other occasions, let the toddler have the large button and hide it in one of his hands. Then you guess where the button is hidden. Invite family members to play "Button, Button, Who's Got the Button" as a group game. Pass the button from person to person, until one person keeps it and only pretends to pass it on. Have your toddler guess who has the button.

Encore ....

Toddlers develop dressing skills as a sign of independence. Some toddlers who learn to button and unbutton and can get themselves dressed and undressed, change clothes several times a day. This habit can be annoying, but keep in mind that it is great fine-motor practice for your toddler. Providing a box of dress-up clothes that your toddler can put on over his clothes will sometimes give a toddler the opportunity to "change" clothes without really changing. Dressing up in Grandma's hat or Grandpa's old shirt is the beginning of make-believe play. Provide a box of easy-to-put-on clothes for your toddler's fantasy play, such as scarves, capes, belts, boots, and hats.

Look, Look

Look, look, and you will see—
A ladybug and a bumble bee.

Overture

Watch your toddler turning the pages of a book. Whereas just a month or two ago she turned several pages at once, now she can turn one page of a book at a time. Soon she will be able to manipulate the pages more freely with one hand and alternate the turning from one hand to the other.

Performance

Play: To help your two-year-old practice turning the pages of a book or magazine, play "Look, Look."
What you will need: Large picture book
How to play: Put the toddler in your lap, facing the book. Hold the book where she can see the pictures and reach the pages. As you read, talk about turning each page. Demonstrate how to lightly touch the top corner of the right-hand page. Demonstrate how to put index finger behind the page and thumb on the corner and hold the page; then pull it gently to the other side of the book. Guide your toddler's hand in turning pages. Then ask your toddler to turn the page. Read the story and each time you need a page turned, ask your toddler to turn the page for you. You might decide together on a special sound that means "turn the page."

Finale

Use another version of the rhyme to play a game. While looking at pictures in a book, use the first line of the rhyme. Then name something on that page. Invite your toddler to point to the thing you named. If the game is too difficult at first, point to the object after you have named it.
Examples:

Look, look, and you will see,
A picture of a *baby bear.*

Look, look, and you will see,
A *flower* under a tree.

Encore

The desire of a two-year-old to listen as an adult reads is a real phenomenon. Your toddler's desire to look at books and hear stories can become one of the greatest teaching tools available to you. Provide age-appropriate board books for your toddler to play independently. Older toddlers prefer simple pictures with few details and bright primary colors. Appropriate books for toddlers to look at individually as well as having the stories read to them include pop-up books and beginning "dress-me" books. Although some of these books are fragile, toddlers also like books with pictures hidden behind moveable windows or doors.

Heigh, Diddle, Diddle

Heigh, diddle, diddle, the cat and the fiddle,
The cow jumped over the moon.
The little dog laughed to see such sport,
And the dish ran away with the spoon.
—Traditional Rhyme

Overture

Watch your toddler eating when he is hungry, and you will see how motivated he can be to perform this fine motor task. Some toddlers are able to feed themselves independently and do not want help. Other children this age must be patiently fed. As the third year progresses, encourage your toddler to feed himself because eating is especially good practice for eye-hand coordination.

Performance

Play: To help your toddler learn how to drink from a cup and eat with a spoon, give him plenty of opportunities to feed himself.

What you will need: Child-sized bowl, spoon, and fork; raisins, round dry cereal, or other bite-sized food, cup of milk

How to play: Seat your toddler in his high chair or the place where he eats. Put a bowl of raisins, a spoon, and cup of milk on the tray or table in front of your toddler. Make it a game to put a raisin on the spoon and lift it to the toddler's mouth without spilling. Practice drinking from the cup, beginning with small amounts of milk. Show your toddler how to place the eating utensils back on the tray.

Finale

Use the rhyme as an action game to practice eating hot cereal. Example:
Heigh, diddle, diddle, (*Dip the spoon into the oatmeal.*)
The cat and the fiddle, (*Hold up the spoonful of cereal.*)
The cow jumped over the moon. (*Lift the spoon up and over like the cow jumping over the moon, and then put it into the toddler's mouth.*)
The little dog laughed (*Smile while your toddler chews.*)
To see such sport, (*Wait for your toddler to swallow.*)
And the dish ran away with the spoon. (*Place the spoon back in the bowl of oatmeal, pick it up, and put it behind your back.*)

Encore

One way to encourage your toddler to use a cup is to let him choose his own special cup. Make the trip to the store to buy his cup a big event. After he chooses the cup and you take it home, show it to the rest of the family with great fanfare. Put it in a place where he can reach it when he wants to show you that he needs a drink.

To Market, to Market

To market, to market to buy a plum bun,
Home again, home again, marketing is done.
—Traditional Rhyme

Overture

Watch your toddler playing with her toys, and you will see that she is beginning to play in a more sophisticated way. During the next year, much of her play will be accompanied by words. She will especially like to pretend she is doing adult tasks including shopping, household chores, and caring for a baby.

Performance

Play: To help your toddler learn how to put things into a bag and take them out again, play "To Market, to Market."

What you will need: Lunch-size paper bags, plastic toy foods or small empty food containers such as yogurt cartons, mini cereal boxes, spice tins, etc.

How to play: Set up an area as the "market." Put the bags and food where your toddler can reach them. Begin by being the "shopper." Choose several items and have your toddler put them in a bag for you. Then let your toddler be the shopper and you put the items in the bag for her.

Finale

Use a different version of the rhyme to play another game. You will need some pieces of real fruit and lunch bags. Replace the words "plum bun" in the rhyme with the name of one of the fruits you are using. After reciting the verse, help the toddler look for that item and place it in a bag. Example:

> To market, to market to buy a *banana,*
> Home again, home again, marketing is done.

Soon your toddler will be able to find the specified fruit and place it in a bag. On other occasions, recite the rhyme when you are going to the market or buying buns in a bakery.

Encore

Foods are highly motivating tools for teaching children. Use daily tasks as learning experiences for your child. For example: unloading groceries from grocery bags can be very enjoyable for your toddler. Place bags of groceries on a table, and let your toddler stand on a chair so she can reach the bags. Encourage her to help you take out the foods and place them on the table. Name each of the foods. Describe the contents of cans and bags. Let your toddler feel how *cold* the frozen foods are and how *heavy* some big cans are. Let her smell the *delicious* aromas of fresh fruits and vegetables. Engaging your toddler's five senses will make her learning more personal and permanent.

Pick Up

One for the money, two for the show,
Three to make ready, and four to go.
—Traditional Rhyme

Overture

Watch two-year-olds playing, and you will see a wide variety of abilities. Toddlers are unpredictable individuals. Some perform activities much earlier or much later than others their age. Trust that your toddler is progressing at exactly ight speed for him.

Performance

Play: To encourage your two-year-old to put toys in a box or container, play "Pick Up."
What you will need: Toys and a toy box or container large enough to hold the toys
How to play: Depending on the desire and ability of your two-year-old, picking up toys can be both fun and educational. You can turn it into a game by placing a certain number of toys on the floor beside the toy box or container. As you name a certain toy, your toddler is to place that particular toy in the container. Example: "Put the teddy bear in the box." When the child puts the toy in the box, applaud or verbally praise him. If he puts a different toy in the box, say something like this: "Good, you put the *block* in the box. I will put the *teddy bear* in the box." As you put each toy in the box, name the toy. Repeat this process as you teach the child the names of other toys, too.

Finale

Use the rhyme to practice listening skills. Tell your child, "When I say 'go,' pick up the blocks and put them in the box." Then recite the rhyme. After the child has mastered picking up his own toys, use the rhyme as a signal to begin the chore.

Encore

On other occasions, use the rhyme whenever your toddler is reluctant to do things including:

◆ Take a bath—If he doesn't want to get into the bath, use the rhyme to challenge him to get undressed quickly.

◆ Get out of the bath—If he does not want to get out of the bathtub, you can use the rhyme to turn it into a race. Say, "When I say 'go,' stand up so I can dry you off." Then recite the rhyme. Or say, "When I say, 'go,' I will lift you out of the tub," and recite the rhyme.

◆ Go to bed—If he does not want to get into bed say, "When I say 'go,' we will put on your pajamas." Recite the rhyme. Then say, "When I say 'go,' run to your bed." Recite the rhyme again.

Keeping Track

Milestone	Date	Comments
Trys to hold a pencil in position for writing		
Can draw lines and circles		
Build block towers		
Can turn a knob to open a door		
Can push to close a door		
Can screw and unscrew jar lids		
Can take off and put on socks		
Can take off shoes		
Can unzip a large zipper		
Can unbutton a large button		
Turns pages of a book one at time		
Drinks from a cup and eats with a spoon		
Puts things in paper bags and takes them out		
Can put toys in a box or container		

Play, Baby, Play

Gross Motor Development

Contemplate

Most two-year-olds are constantly on the move—running, kicking, climbing, jumping, hopping, rolling, moving every which way. Toddlers just naturally celebrate their marvelous gross motor development. Children this age love piggyback rides, wrestling, rolling on mats, and climbing on age-appropriate playground equipment.

Although most two-year-olds have been walking for some time, it is during this third year of life that they master these movements. Your toddler will become more self-confident in his movements and no longer have to concentrate so hard on each step he takes. Two-year-olds can walk and perform gross motor tasks at the same time. Watch during the year, and you will notice that your two-year-old is mastering many new gross motor skills.

Giving your toddler large muscle exercise is essential to attain this level of development. Help your toddler learn to walk forward and backward, balance on one foot, walk on tiptoe, lie on his back and "pedal" in the air, turn around, jump over things, and jump down from things. All of these movements are good practice for balance. More specifically, the games in this chapter will help you introduce and reinforce age-appropriate gross motor milestones.

Gross Motor Milestones: 24 to 36 Months

◆ Will learn the heel-to-toe motion in walking
◆ Will learn how to stand on tiptoes
◆ Will learn to carry things while walking
◆ Will learn to move freely with rhythm (marching)
◆ Will learn to hold hands while moving around in a circle
◆ Will learn how to gallop
◆ Will learn to walk up and down stairs with alternating feet (while holding onto a railing)
◆ Will learn to step up and down from a step stool
◆ Will learn to pedal a tricycle and/or other pedal toys
◆ Will learn how to bend over to retrieve objects from the floor without tumbling down
◆ Will learn to kick a large stationary ball
◆ Will learn to roll and toss a ball
◆ Will enjoy playing on playground equipment
◆ Will use his whole body to play action games
◆ Will use his whole body to move in free ways

 General Tips

Two-year-olds generally have *energy spurts* that are hard to follow. The good news is, you do not have to keep up with them. Children this age do not usually need guidance in developing motor skills. They do that all by themselves. But since a two-year-old has little self-control and her judgment lags considerably behind her gross motor skills, you will need to keep constant vigilance. In the next few months, safety and preventing injuries will be your most important contribution to your toddler's gross motor development.

You do not have to own all of the equipment needed for gross motor practice. A nearby park, playground, or schoolyard will provide the equipment your toddler needs for practicing large muscle activities. Join in the fun by helping her play on the playground equipment—especially the slides and swings.

Moving with rhythm and grace can be reinforced by providing music, singing songs, reciting rhymes, dancing, marching, running, and playing movement games with your toddler. Engaging in physical play with your toddler will be enjoyable and great exercise for you. Set aside plenty of time each day when your toddler can go outside to play. The high level of energy that a two-year-old has must be spent each day. To ask a toddler to sit quietly in front of a television or remain in a small confined space would be detrimental to her gross motor development. If weather does not permit outdoor play every day, provide a large safe area indoors for movement activities. Take walks in indoor malls, school gyms, at play-group gatherings, etc.

Have faith in your toddler's natural capacity to gain gross motor skills. *Resist the urge to push or force growth.* Instead, find a seat in the shade of a tree where you can supervise her play. It will be a pleasure to observe the miracle of your toddler strengthening her own body and developing good coordination naturally, during her active play.

Be physical with your toddler. Toddlers this age love *rough and tumble play.* She will enjoy racing and playing tag. And do not forget the best exercise of all—grasping and hugging someone with giant bear hugs!

One Foot Up, One Foot Down

See-saw, sacaradown, sacaradown.
Which is the way to London town?
One foot up, and the other foot down.
That is the way to London town.
—Traditional Rhyme

Overture

Toddlers are highly geared to gross motor activity. They love to romp, lug, tug, push, and pull. With this new and greater coordination comes an opportunity for rhythmic fun and dance.

Performance

Play: To reinforce your toddler's heel-to-toe motion in walking, play "One Foot Up, One Foot Down."

What you will need: Room to march, marching music

How to play: Play some marching music, and show your toddler how to march with the rhythm of the music. If he is too young to move with the beat, that is okay; it will come in time. Lift your knees high. Place one foot in front of other foot and march around the room. Take turns being the leader.

Finale

Use the rhyme to march to the beat of the rhythm in the verse. Which foot leads right or left is not important; the important thing is to alternate feet in a marching style. Your toddler probably will not be able to keep a beat in the early months of the third year, but as he gets close to age three, marching to a beat will be easy for him. Try using this version of the rhyme to march.
Example:
　　See-saw (*right/left*), up and down (*right/left*).
　　Which is the way (*right/left*) to London town (*right/left*)?
　　One foot up (*right/left*), the other foot down (*right/left*),
　　That's the way (*right/left*) to London town (*right/left*).

Encore

On other occasions, use various versions of the rhyme to march to lunch, to bed, to the bathtub, etc. Change the word "London" to the place where you are headed.
Example:
　　See-saw, up and down.
　　Which way is our *lunch* (bath, bed) be found?
　　One foot up, and the other foot down.
　　Where is the kitchen (bathtub, bedroom, etc.) to be found?
Children this age enjoy using rhythm instruments when marching and CD's or audiotapes of marching music.

Reach and Touch the Moon

Stretch up to the moon.
Reach and touch the sky.
Can I tap a star?
I can, if I try.

Overture

Toddlers this age are fascinated by words and word play. They especially enjoy rhymes because rhymes are stories with rhythm and repetitive sounds. Children often enjoy repeating a rhyme until they master it. Recite rhymes as you exercise and move.

Performance

Play: To practice standing on tiptoes, play "Reach and Touch the Moon."
What you will need: No special equipment is needed to play this game.
How to play: For good coordination practice, play stretching games. Stand facing your toddler. Demonstrate how to reach and stretch toward the sky. Say, "Stretch up to the clouds. Reach and touch the sky." Then tell the toddler to "rest," and demonstrate how to relax and stand flat-footed again. Repeat.

Finale

Use the rhyme to do the following exercise:
 Stretch up to the moon. (*Stretch hands in the air above head.*)
 Reach and touch the sky. (*Stand on tiptoes and stretch upwards.*)
 Can you tap a star? (*Use hands to tap an imaginary star.*)
 I can, if I try. (*Bring arms down and stand flat-footed.*)

Or try variations of the rhyme:
 Stretch up to the ceiling. (*On tiptoes, stretch hands in the air above head.*)
 Reach and touch the wall. (*Reach hands out straight to the sides.*)
 Can I tap that window? (*Put hands out straight to the front.*)
 I can, if I try. (*Bring arms down and stand flat-footed.*)

 Stretch down to the floor. (*Bend at the waist.*)
 Reach and touch your knees. (*Reach down and touch knees.*)
 Can I tap the floor? (*Place hands flat on the floor.*)
 I can, if I try. (*Tap the floor with flat hands.*)

Encore

On other occasions, play a stretching game. As you mention a body part, touch it. Have your toddler do the same. Begin very slowly. As your toddler learns the game, say the rhyme more and more quickly until your toddler has to perform the touches at a very fast pace.
Example:
 Head and shoulders, knees and toes, knees and toes. (*Repeat.*)
 Eyes and ears and mouth and nose,
 Head and shoulders, knees and toes, knees and toes.

Grab a Pig

Tom, Tom, the piper's son,
Grabbed a pig and away he run.

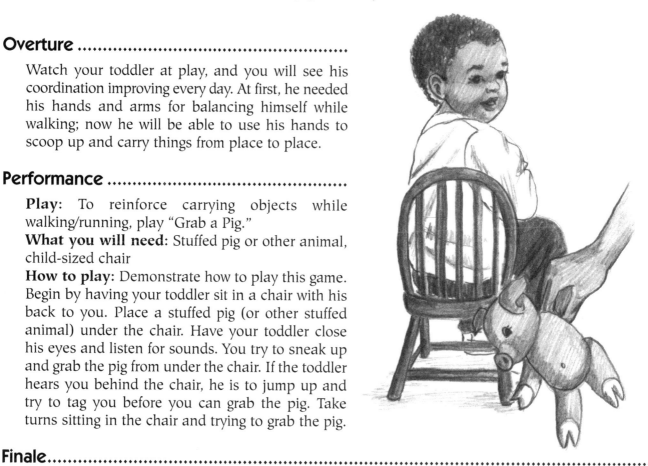

Overture ....

Watch your toddler at play, and you will see his coordination improving every day. At first, he needed his hands and arms for balancing himself while walking; now he will be able to use his hands to scoop up and carry things from place to place.

Performance ....

Play: To reinforce carrying objects while walking/running, play "Grab a Pig."
What you will need: Stuffed pig or other animal, child-sized chair
How to play: Demonstrate how to play this game. Begin by having your toddler sit in a chair with his back to you. Place a stuffed pig (or other stuffed animal) under the chair. Have your toddler close his eyes and listen for sounds. You try to sneak up and grab the pig from under the chair. If the toddler hears you behind the chair, he is to jump up and try to tag you before you can grab the pig. Take turns sitting in the chair and trying to grab the pig.

Finale...

Play the game while reciting the verse. On the words "grabbed a pig" your toddler should try to grab the pig from under the chair and run. Jump up quickly and run after your toddler. If interested, recite a version of the rhyme while playing a new game. Line up a variety of stuffed animals. Replace the word "pig" with the name of another animal in the line. When you name one of the animals, your toddler should choose that toy and run with it.
Examples:

(Toddler's name), (toddler's name), the piper's son (daughter),
Grabbed a *bear* and away he (she) run.

Encore...

On other occasions, ask the toddler to carry light-weight objects for you.
   ◆ If traveling, give your toddler a small pillow or bag to carry.
   ◆ When shopping, ask your toddler to carry an object around the store for you.
   ◆ When bringing the groceries into your home, ask your toddler to carry one of the items.
   ◆ When working in the yard, ask your toddler to move armloads of leaves for you.
   ◆ When leaving the library, ask your toddler to carry one book to the car.

Here We Go Round

Here we go round the mulberry bush,
The mulberry bush, the mulberry bush.
Here we go round the mulberry bush,
On a cold and frosty morning.
　　　　　　　　—Traditional Rhyme

Overture

Another kind of experimentation that plays a dominant role at this age involves body movement. Watch your toddler moving about, and you will see her practicing thrust and acceleration.

Performance

Play: To encourage your toddler to move freely with rhythm, play "Here We Go Round."
What you will need: Jazz music
How to play: Hold the child's hands or carry her so she can get the feel of the beat. Dance and prance (move in a flowing movement—not stepping or marching) to the sound of music. Keep time to the music so she will feel the rhythm. Enjoy and flow with the sound.

Finale

Use the rhyme to introduce household objects or common things found in the yard. Dance around chanting new words to the verse.
Examples:

　Here we go round the dining room table,
　The dining room table, the dining room table.
　Here we go round the dining room table,
　On a cold and frosty morning.

　Here we go round the giant oak tree,
　The giant oak tree, the giant oak tree.
　Here we go round the giant oak tree,
　On a cold and frosty morning.

Encore

On other occasions—during different seasons—change the last line of the rhyme to sing about the weather and time of day.
Examples:
   ◆ On a hot and breezy morning
   ◆ On a wet and rainy afternoon
   ◆ On a foggy and cold night
   ◆ On a snowy Christmas day
   ◆ On (toddler's name)'s birthday.

Gallop-a-Trot

This is the way the girls ride! Gallop-a-trot, gallop-a-trot!
This is the way the boys ride! Gallop-a-trot, gallop-a-trot!

Overture

Shared physical activities have the qualities of games. Although there are no winners or losers, there are unspoken rules that define a toddler's games. Even a rough-and-tumble wrestling match has unspoken rules about the roles the parent and child will play. When your toddler learns a game, he will remember the rules and roles even if the game is not played every day.

Performance

Play: To help introduce and reinforce the galloping movement, play "Gallop-a-Trot."
What you will need: No special equipment is needed to play this game.
How to play: The term "gallop" comes from the way a horse runs. Gallop means to lead with one leg. Demonstrate a gallop (run leading with the right foot). Then gallop leading with the left foot.

Finale

Use the nursery rhyme "Little Hobby Horse" and a stick horse to help your toddler learn how to gallop around the house or yard:

I had a little hobby horse,
And it was dapple gray.
Its head was made of pea-straw;
Its tail was made of hay.

Use galloping as a way to move in games: run galloping races, play galloping tag, and gallop all around the house. Give a variety of instructions:

◆ Gallop around that tree and back.
◆ Gallop all the way around the house.
◆ Gallop to your bed.

Encore

On other occasions, have the toddler try to move backward. Include exercises such as:
◆ Walk backward.
◆ Try running backward.
◆ Hop back one step.
◆ March backward.
◆ Tiptoe backward.

Upstairs and Downstairs

Wee Willie Winkie, runs through the town,
Upstairs and downstairs, in his nightgown, . . .
—Traditional Rhyme

Overture

Watch, and you will see that your toddler is virtually fearless. On stairs, she could easily hurtle herself through space. Teach your toddler how to use stairs either by crawling on tummy or by stepping up one step at a time while you hold onto her hand.

Performance

Play: To practice walking up and down stairs with alternating feet, play "Upstairs and Downstairs."

What you will need: Stairs with a handrail

How to play: Show your toddler how to hold on to the handrail with one hand. Hold her other hand and slowly move up the stairs. Work on learning to climb up. Make sure your toddler feels confident going up the stairs before you begin to teach how to walk down the stairs. Walking down is much more difficult and must be accomplished slowly. In the beginning, her climbing may be stiff-legged, but as your toddler gains more confidence, a heel-to-toe motion will take over. Just for fun, use the rhyme sometimes when you practice walking upstairs. After the toddler has confidence climbing up and down the stairs, take the stairs instead of elevators when using public buildings. Always use handrails, and explain to your toddler that stairs are not a place to play.

Finale

Once your toddler is a good stair climber, it is appropriate for her to have her own step stool in the bathroom. It will make washing hands and brushing teeth easier. Your toddler will most likely be learning to use the toilet this year, and so she will need a step stool to wash and dry her hands independently.

Encore

A step stool with one step and a wide landing, light enough so your toddler can move it around will make self-care in the bathroom easier. The toddler can use the stool to reach the water faucets when washing hands and brushing teeth. She will be able to stand on it and see herself when washing her face and combing her hair. Before giving a toddler a step stool, practice safe ways of stepping up and down. See the directions for teaching your toddler how to use a step stool on the following page.

Up and Down

Up, up, up. Down, down, down.
Up and down. Walk around.

Overture

Watch your toddler lift one foot off the floor and remain balanced long enough to place that foot on a step. What takes great whole body coordination and total mental concentration for a 24-month-old will become second nature by the time he is 36 months old.

Performance

Play: To help your toddler learn how to climb up and down on a step stool, play "Up and Down."
What you will need: Step stool with only one step
How to play: Place the step stool on floor between you and your toddler. Demonstrate how to step up onto the stool. Then show him how to step off. Instruct the toddler to "step up" and "step down." Practice stepping up and down. Continue until your toddler can perform the motion smoothly.

Finale

Use the rhyme and the stool as an action game.
Example:

 Up, up, up. (*Step up on the stool.*)
 Down, down, down. (*Step down from the stool.*)
 Up, up; down, down. (*Step up; step down.*)
 Walk around. (*Walk around the stool.*)

Play music and hold the toddler's hands. Incorporate his moving up and down on the step stool into part of a little dance. Every day, encourage your toddler to dance while you watch. Find a place in your home where a lighted spot can become your toddler's stage. Take your seat in the "front row" and enjoy the show of your lifetime.

Encore

A more intense kind of exploration occurs when two-year-old children investigate the spatial layout of their immediate environment. Toddlers love to walk along a wide wall while holding onto one hand of parent. Two-year-olds seem to search out balance beams for practicing their newly acquired skill—walking. Create a ramp with an 18- to 24-inch (46- to 61-cm) wide plank and place it flat on the floor to provide your toddler with an opportunity to explore and test his balance. Also, drawing parallel lines 12 inches (31 cm) apart on the sidewalk with chalk will give your toddler an imaginary beam to test his balance.

114

Get Set, Go!

On your mark,
Get set,
Go!

Overture

Watch your toddler this year, and you will see that her musculoskeletal system continues to be the one with the greatest growth. She will continue to show steady improvement in the quality of her motor activities. The arm and leg coordination that enables a two-year-old to run and jump can now be applied to riding a tricycle.

Performance

Play: To help your toddler practice getting onto and pedaling a tricycle or pushing ride-on toys with her feet, play "Get Set, Go!"

What you will need: Small tricycle (with wide wheel base for stability) or other small pedal toy, green scarf or flag

How to play: Ask the toddler to stand on a spot near the tricycle. Use the rhyme as follows:

On your mark, (*Toddler runs to tricycle.*)
Get set, (*Toddler gets on the tricycle.*)
Go! (*Wave the scarf or flag as your toddler rides off.*)

Most toddlers truly enjoy these three steps to beginning a ride. Repeat the racing game as long as your toddler shows interest.

Finale

Use the rhyme to begin rides on ride-on push toys. Children's interest in vehicles will continue to grow during this year. Toddlers like realistic replicas of vehicles or animals; rocking horses and pedal cars are favorites.

Encore

On other occasions, use the rhyme to begin races that involve pushing or pulling. A small wagon is a good toy for a toddler. A toddler can lean on it, pull it, or fill it with stuff. Toys that have handles such as doll carriages and miniature shopping carts are great for practicing pushing. Encourage the toddler to try pushing fairly heavy objects such as a chair or large box. Also use the rhyme to begin tag games. Children this age love to run and will enjoy it even more if they are being chased by someone. Remember, turnabout is fair play—let her chase you, too.

You Can Catch It

*Rowley, Rowley, pudding and pie,
You can catch it, if you try.*

Overture

Watch your toddler and you will see that he may still be unable to dart about rapidly or make quick turns. This is the year he will probably learn to ride a tricycle and catch a moving ball. Throwing is a gross motor skill that often develops dramatically between the ages of two and three.

Performance

Play: To help your toddler learn how to bend down and recover objects from the floor without tumbling over, play "You Can Catch It."

What you will need: Tennis ball or small beach ball

How to play: While standing up, roll a tennis ball across the floor and invite your toddler to go after it. Ask the toddler to roll it back to you. Then roll it to him again. Tennis balls are soft enough that toddlers can easily grasp them. This game will also provide your toddler practice with his pincher grasp.

Finale

Use the rhyme to play a sitting down ball game. Sit about 6 feet (2 meters) from your toddler. Spread apart your legs and show your toddler how to do the same. Recite the rhyme as you roll the ball toward him. Then have him roll it back again.

Play standing and sitting ball games with a variety of balls and equipment. Try a bowling game, use empty soda bottles as bowling pins. Your toddler can try to knock them down with any of the following:

- ◆ Big round ball
- ◆ Beach ball
- ◆ Small rubber ball
- ◆ Youth-sized basketball

Have the toddler try to catch a beach ball or inflated balloon. With the increasing coordination of his gross motor actions during this third year, your toddler will be able to focus on a target while rolling or catching. He will enjoy playing with balls of all sizes.

Encore

On other occasions, use beanbags as great tossing toys. Set up targets drawn on the sidewalk with chalk or use large laundry baskets. How many beanbags can he throw into the basket in one minute? Toss and retrieve, toss and retrieve, until time is called.

Kick Ball

Billy, Billy, come and play,
While the sun shines bright as day.
—Traditional Rhyme

Overture

Watch your toddler, and you will see that she prefers toys that move. Balls are especially interesting toys because they bounce, roll, and move about in unexpected ways. Whereas it is usually not a good idea to kick toys, kicking a ball is appropriate. Toddlers like to cause balls to move quickly in new directions.

Performance

Play: To give your toddler practice kicking a large stationary ball, play "Kick Ball."
What you will need: Large rubber ball
How to play: Have the toddler kick the ball and then run to retrieve it. Place the ball back down in front of her. Repeat the steps.

Finale

Use masking tape or chalk to draw a line where the ball came to rest. Continue kicking the ball and marking the distance it traveled. How far can your toddler kick the ball? Then try using targets and kicking the ball in particular directions. For example:
- ◆ Kick the ball so it touches a garage door.
- ◆ Kick the ball to another person.

Try kicking a variety of balls such as a foam ball, tennis ball, soccer ball, or football.

For great coordination practice, try kicking things besides balls.
- ◆ Scoot beanbags along the floor with the foot.
- ◆ Kick small boxes around the lawn.
- ◆ Kick an inflated balloon high into the air.
- ◆ Scoot a pair of rolled-up socks to the bedroom.
- ◆ Kick a paper wad around a table.

Encore

Instead of using the foot to kick a ball, use a variety of objects to move the ball including:
- ◆ Plastic tennis racket
- ◆ Table tennis paddle
- ◆ Fly swatter
- ◆ Fat plastic bat

Catch!

Catch the ball.
Snatch the ball.

Overture

Watch toddlers trying to catch balls, and you will see a variety of techniques. Some will stop the ball by letting it hit them in the chest and then grasp it with both arms. Other toddlers can stop a ball with one hand and grab it with the other. Still others will stop it with a hand and push it against their bodies to catch it. Stopping a moving ball and catching it takes a great deal of coordination and skill. It is something your toddler will need practice to learn.

Performance

Play: To help your toddler learn how to roll and toss a ball to another person, play "Catch."
What you will need: A large, rubber ball such as a beach ball
How to play: Stand facing your toddler about 3 feet (1 meter) apart. Have him extend his arms ready to catch the ball. Carefully toss the ball into his arms and say, "Catch!" Toss gently so the ball will land on extended arms, making it easier to catch. Ask the toddler to throw the ball back to you. Catching and tossing a ball is very difficult. Begin slowly and take your time. So that the game does not become too frustrating, play only as long as your toddler is interested in learning to catch and toss.

Finale

Practice tossing and catching with a variety of things besides balls including:

◆ Small pillow
◆ Large beanbag
◆ Large inflated balloon
◆ Feathers
◆ Paper airplane
◆ Paper wad
◆ Stuffed bear
◆ Silk scarf
◆ Large bath sponge

Encore

Without any formal instruction, just by playing with balls, your toddler will master techniques needed for games of sport. Attending sports events and taking your toddler to parks and school athletic events to watch the games will give him an opportunity to observe how balls and sports equipment are used, how players move, and how team members cooperate.

Swinging

Swing up my darling, swing him up high,
Don't let his head, though, hit the blue sky.

Overture

Although pedaling a tricycle and pumping a swing requires a similar kind of coordination, children usually learn to ride tricycles long before they can pump swings. You can show your toddler how to pump himself on the swing, but do not count on him being willing to swing unless you push him. It is just more fun that way.

Performance

Play: Swinging is a relaxing activity that children usually enjoy together. To teach your toddler how to use playground equipment, especially swings, visit playgrounds often.

What you will need: Swing made with soft and flexible materials

How to play: Insist that the toddler sit in the middle of the seat and hold on with both hands. Stand behind your toddler and push gently. Begin very slowly, making sure the toddler enjoys the sensation of swinging. When you want to teach your toddler how to pump a swing so he can propel himself back and forth, demonstrate what to do while he watches. Then put him in the swing and talk him through the steps.

- ◆ While swinging backward, tuck legs up under the body and lean forward slightly.
- ◆ When moving forward, push legs straight out in front and lean backward.

Have him try the steps as you verbally guide him.

Finale

Teach your toddler swing rules for safety:

- ◆ Always hold on with both hands.
- ◆ Never walk in front of or behind a swing while another youngster is on it.
- ◆ Two children are never to share the same swing.
- ◆ Do not get off the swing until it has completely stopped.
- ◆ Never stand up or do tricks on a swing.

Encore

On other occasions, help your toddler learn how to properly use other playground equipment.

- ◆ Teeter-totters—Are not appropriate for toddlers. They do not have the arm and leg coordination to use them.
- ◆ Jungle gyms—Never let your toddler use equipment that is taller than he is without close supervision.
- ◆ Slides—Never let your toddler climb up the sliding surface. Always use the stairs to get to the top. Check the surface to see if it is hot before sliding down. When the toddler reaches the bottom of the slide, he should quickly move away from the slide to avoid being hit in the back by the next person who slides down.

I'm a Little Teapot

I'm a little teapot, short and stout.
This is my handle, this is my spout.
When my water boils, I begin to shout,
"Tip me up and pour me out."
—Traditional Rhyme

Overture

Action games help children develop skills using their whole bodies. Play games that will challenge your toddler to use several parts of her body at once.

Performance

Play: To help your toddler learn how to use her arms and legs together, play "I'm a Little Teapot."
What you will need: No special equipment is needed to play this game.
How to play: Demonstrate the actions for the rhyme. Repeat, inviting the toddler to join you. Your toddler will soon learn the actions to the rhyme and will be able to do them independently.

I'm a little teapot, (*Stand up tall on tiptoes.*)
Short and stout. (*Put feet flat on floor.*)
This is my handle, (*Curve right arm and touch waist to make a handle.*)
This is my spout. (*Hold left arm up with hand tipped out to make spout.*)
When my water boils, (*Wiggle fingers as if water is boiling.*)
I begin to shout, (*Put hands to mouth as if shouting.*)
"Tip me up (*Pretend body is a tipped teapot.*)
and pour me out." (*Take a low bow from the waist.*)

Finale

Use other rhymes as finger plays.
Example:
Eye winker, (*Wink one eye.*)
Tom thinker, (*Point to temple.*)
Nose dropper, (*Squeeze nostrils.*)
Mouth eater, (*Pretend to chew.*)
Chin chopper, (*Strike chin playfully.*)
Chin chopper. (*Strike chin playfully again.*)

Encore

Create actions using different body parts for familiar rhymes like "Little Boy Blue," "Mary Had a Little Lamb," and "Little Jack Horner." Personalize the verses by putting in your toddler's name. Be creative.

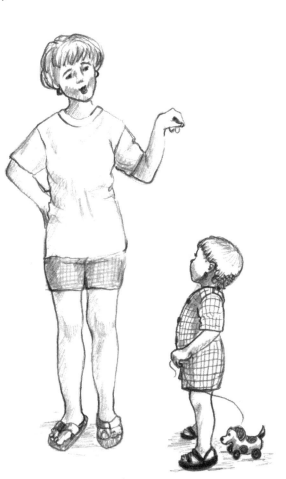

Little (toddler's name) Blue, come blow your horn.
The sheep's in the meadow, the cow's in the corn.

(Toddler's name) had a little (toy/pet).
Little (toy/pet), little (toy/pet).
(Toddler's name) had a little (toy/pet).
She liked to play with it best.

Look! I'm a Cloud

Hush-a-by, baby, over the tree tops,
When the wind blows, the clouds will flow.

Overture ....

During the third year, your toddler's movements will evolve from jerky and uncoordinated to smooth and flowing. Since toddlers enjoy pretending to be things they see around them, like animals or objects in nature, use make-believe to practice moving the whole body.

Performance ....

Play: To encourage the toddler to use her whole body to move in free ways, play "Look! I'm a Cloud."

What you will need: Four silk scarves, windy day with clouds

How to play: Begin this activity by lying flat on your back in the grass with your toddler. Watch the wind-blown clouds moving across the sky. Talk about how it might feel to float above the trees like a cloud. Then tie a scarf around each of your toddler's wrists and one around each of your own. Move in the breeze like a cloud flowing across the sky. Try these variations, too:

- ◆ The wind stops blowing and the clouds stay very still.
- ◆ The wind blows hard and the clouds are blown every which way.
- ◆ A whirlwind catches the clouds and spins them round and round.
- ◆ The clouds are heavy with rain, and rain begins to fall from them.

Finale ....

Play classical music as you move. Use scarves, pinwheels, bubbles, or other props to enhance your dancing. Try slow music and then fast music. Use music that has varied tones, pitch, and rhythm such as Beethoven's *Moonlight Sonata.*

Encore ....

On other occasions, pretend to be other natural objects such as:

- ◆ A leaf being blown by the wind, then falling from the tree, floating to the ground, blowing around on the ground
- ◆ A baby bird very slowly hatching from an egg
- ◆ A butterfly emerging from a cocoon
- ◆ A flower budding, blooming, and then dropping seeds

        121

Follow My Lead

Follow my lead. Do what I do,
Run, jump, hop. Gallop, leap. Stop!

Overture

Exploring space and moving about can be a leisurely process for two-year-olds. Often they do not want to move at an adult's pace. If you find that your toddler does not like to play games with your rules or at your hurried pace, let him guide you and see if changing the speed of the game will get him to participate with a new level of enthusiasm.

Performance

Play: To reinforce all of the gross motor movements your toddler has learned, play "Follow My Lead."

What you will need: No special equipment is needed to play this game.

How to play: Stand facing the toddler. Use the rhyme and move in special ways including:

- ◆ Walk heel-to-toe
- ◆ March
- ◆ Run in place
- ◆ Jump

Invite your toddler to follow your lead and do what you do. Then stop. Then repeat the lines and move in a new way. Say something like this, "That is right. We are hopping." After you have been the leader for awhile, give your toddler a chance to be the leader.

Finale

Use rhymes or music and do each movement as you name it. Then let your toddler demonstrate a movement and you follow him. Exercising to music is fun and provides a great outlet for expending energy for toddlers. Short segments of aerobic programs on television are sometimes enjoyed by youngsters.

Encore

To coordinate the movements of her hands and feet, have your toddler use rhythm instruments with her hands while using his legs and feet to walk, run, jump, hop, leap, and gallop.

Keeping Track

Milestone	Date	Comments
Can walk with a heel-to-toe motion		
Can march		
Can stand on tiptoes		
Can carry things while walking		
Can move freely with rhythm (march)		
Can jump		
Can gallop		
Can walk up and down the stairs		
Can step up and down from a step stool		
Can pedal a tricycle or other pedal toys		
Can pick up objects without tumbling over		
Can kick a large stationary ball		
Can roll and toss a ball		
Enjoys playground equipment		
Can use body to play action games		
Can use body to move in free ways		
Can perform a variety of movements		

Let's Talk

Language Development

 Contemplate

Your toddler's language development during his third year will probably amaze you. Many children this age begin to speak in sentences which include verbs. Some begin using adjectives and adverbs: "pretty," "big," "good," "very," etc. It is believed that often girls develop language skills more quickly than do boys. During their preschool years, youngsters may master many words or hardly speak at all. Do not be alarmed if your toddler seems slow in developing language skills. You can encourage all of his attempts to speak by being a patient listener.

Toddlers often stammer or stutter while speaking. This is a normal part of learning to form words. This stage of language development is not a good time for correcting your child. Finding fault in your toddler's speech might cause her to become reluctant to express herself. Some speech therapist think that at two years of age, children should no longer hear "baby talk." Others disagree and feel that the use of some "baby talk" signals the toddler that you are speaking just to him. Only you will know the best time to use adult speech exclusively with your toddler. Use the games in this chapter to introduce and reinforce skills needed to master the language milestones below.

Language Milestones: 24 to 36 Months

- ◆ Will be able to mimic most sounds heard
- ◆ Will begin to respond verbally to things he sees around him
- ◆ Will learn to sing simple songs
- ◆ Will learn to make the sounds that some animals make
- ◆ Will learn to recognize and name most common objects
- ◆ Will learn to obey a two- or three-component request
- ◆ Will learn to speak in four- to six-word sentences
- ◆ Will learn to give his name and age
- ◆ Will learn to use pronouns ("I," "you," "we," "she")
- ◆ Will begin to use plurals correctly ("toys," "balls")
- ◆ Will begin to use adjectives ("red," "blue," "big," "little")
- ◆ Will begin to use adverbs to indicate spatial relationships ("up" and "down")
- ◆ Will begin to use prepositions to indicate spatial relationships ("in," "on," "over," "under")
- ◆ Will learn to repeat nonsense sounds

General Tips

The favorite word for many two-year-olds is "no!" Many parents see a toddler's choosing not to do something as inappropriate behavior. Childhood development specialists disagree; they believe that toddlers need to learn to make choices. Honoring a child's wish demonstrates that you respect her preferences. The important thing is to teach your toddler to distinguish between times when she can choose and times when she cannot choose. Explain to her that if you ask a question, that means she has a choice. However, if you make a statement or give a command, this indicates that she does not have a choice and must obey.
Examples:

◆ Are you ready to go to bed? (Can choose—"yes" or "no.")
◆ It is time for bed. (A command—cannot choose.)

The key will be helping your toddler make the distinction between *questions* and *statements*.

Another favorite word of many two-year-olds is "why?" Your toddler probably asks you dozens or even hundreds of questions every day. Do you sometimes get weary from explaining everything? To a child, the whole world is a mystery. It is excellent that she is curious and wants to know how things work. The only way she can learn is to ask and explore. *You are the master teacher.* Take the time to answer questions. Keep in mind, sometimes we think children are asking something much more complicated than what they are actually trying to understand. When you answer questions, be accurate and use the correct terminology.

As soon as your toddler can talk, encourage her to verbalize her needs, wants, and feelings. When she cries, say something like this: "Instead of crying, tell me what you want." If her tears indicate something she does not want, you might add, "I know what you don't want; tell me what you do want." Helping your toddler verbalize her feelings will teach her how to recognize and communicate her basic needs to others. *Concentrate on warm, friendly communications.* Remember, good rapport is only possible when she knows that you are listening.

Some ways to encourage language development include:

◆ Speak to your toddler, not over her.
◆ Do not rush to meet her every need; give her a chance to verbalize her needs.
◆ Give her opportunities to make choices.
◆ Give her opportunities to experiment and discover answers.

Praise your toddler's every effort to communicate with you. Tell her how proud you are that she can speak. Daily, *reinforce her efforts with kind words* and encouragement.

Language Development 24- to 36-Month-Old

© Instructional Fair • TS Denison **125**

Echo Me

Yankee Doodle went to town upon a little pony.
He stuck a feather in his hat and called it Macaroni.
—Traditional Rhyme

Overture ....

At this stage of her language development, your toddler will benefit from spending a short period with you each day on structured learning—activities that are aimed at teaching specific sounds or words.

Performance ....

Play: To encourage your toddler to mimic the sounds she hears, play "Echo Me."
What you will need: Picture books and magazines with bright pictures
How to play: Look at picture books and magazines with your toddler. Point to familiar and unfamiliar objects. Carefully enunciate the name of each object. Ask your child to repeat each word you say. Along with common objects, include some not-so-familiar objects. For example, if you are looking at a book of zoo animals, introduce the difficult-to-say words such as "rhinoceros," "hippopotamus," and "alligator." Your toddler may not be able to say them, but it is good for her to hear the words while she is looking at the pictures.

Finale ....

Because it has a variety of initial consonants, use the rhyme "Yankee Doodle" as an echo game. Begin by saying one word at a time, and ask your child to echo each word you speak. Then say two or three words at a time as she echoes the words. When appropriate, say an entire line for her to echo. Soon your toddler will be able to say all four lines. Teach her other nursery rhymes using the one-word, two-word, and then a-whole-line method.
Examples:

Rain, rain, go to Spain,
Don't come back again.

It's raining, it's pouring,
The old man is snoring.
(*Make a snoring sound.*)

Encore ....

On other occasions, when you see an interesting object, name the object for your toddler. Then ask, "Can you say that?" No matter how she says the word, respond with praise. If the child repeats the word incorrectly, instead of correcting her simply echo the word correctly. Example: If your child says, "See the *wabbit.*" Do not correct the pronunciation, simply incorporate the correct pronunciation into the conversation. Say something like this: "Yes, I see the *rabbit.*"

Make a Wish

Starlight, star bright, first star I see tonight.
I wish I may, I wish I might, have the wish I wish tonight.
—Traditional Rhyme

Overture

Most adults take for granted the ability to imitate speech, but in reality it is a small miracle. The best way to help your child gain language is to give her many opportunities to see interesting things that she will want to talk about.

Performance

Play: To encourage your toddler to respond verbally to things she sees around her, make a wish on a first star.
What you will need: Warm evening, first evening star shining in the sky
How to play: Locate the first star (Venus) in the evening sky. Venus can usually be seen even before dark. Point out the first star to your toddler. Teach your toddler that wishing for something is the first step in making it happen. When she can visualize something she needs or wants, it might happen. When she tells others about her wish, they might be able or willing to help her make the wish come true.

Finale

Perhaps there is nothing quite as awesome as the night sky. Share this wonder with your toddler. Teach your toddler the rhyme "Starlight, Star Bright." Use it at night to make wishes on the first star.

Encore

When you and your toddler are out in the evenings, look for the first star and use the rhyme to make wishes. Talk to your child about some of the following concepts regarding making wishes:

◆ Sometimes we get what we wish for; especially if we tell someone who loves us—someone who is willing to help us make it happen.
◆ We do not always get everything we wish for.
◆ It is okay to wish for things we do not get.
◆ Bad things do not happen because someone wishes they will happen.
◆ Wishing is visualizing something we want.

Share with your toddler some stories about things you wished for when you were a child. Share the wishes you make today, too.

Sing a Song

I sing, I sing, from morn till night,
From cares I'm free, and my heart is light.
—Traditional Rhyme

Overture

Singing to a two-year-old is a natural way to stimulate his listening skills. Familiar songs with repetitive words and a sing-song rhythm are comforting to toddlers. Personalizing a song will make it more interesting to your toddler.

Performance

Play: To encourage your toddler to sing songs, play "Sing a Song."
What you will need: Music
How to play: Singing the words to easy-to-remember repetitive songs helps young learners develop language skills. Use the song "Happy Birthday" as a beginning song. Then use the same tune to sing variations of the song.

Happy birthday to you, happy birthday to you,
Happy birthday, dear friend, happy birthday to you.

For variations, replace "Happy birthday" with:
- ◆ Good morning   ◆ Good night
- ◆ Best wishes   ◆ Happy day

Finale

Use simple rhymes as songs. The more repetitive and simple the rhymes are, the easier they will be for your toddler to remember and sing. "Mary had a Little Lamb" is a good song to sing and an easy tune to remember.

Mary had a little lamb, little lamb, little lamb.
Mary had a little lamb, its fleece was white as snow.

On other occasions, sing personalized versions of "Mary Had a Little Lamb."
Examples:
- ◆ Lucy had a little kitten, . . . its paws were gray as smoke.
- ◆ Jason had a little bed, . . . its covers were soft as clouds.

Encore

Toddlers enjoy anticipating the end of familiar songs. Try singing songs and pausing so your toddler can finish each line.
Examples:
London Bridge is falling down, falling down, falling down.
London Bridge is falling down, my fair _____ (lady).

One for the money. Two for the show.
Three to make ready and four to _____ (go).

What Sounds Do They Make?

Baa, baa, black sheep, have you any wool?
Yes sir, yes sir, three bags full. . . .
—Traditional Rhyme

Overture

Toddlers especially enjoy songs that they can join in singing. "Old MacDonald Had a Farm" is a good song because as you think of new animals, you will keep adding new words and sounds for your toddler to learn.

Performance

Play: To help your toddler make the sounds some animals make, play "What Sounds Do They Make?"

What you will need: Picture books with pictures of farm animals

How to play: Point to a picture of an animal, and make the sound the animal makes. Look for pictures of these animals to share their sounds with the toddler:

- Lamb—baa, baa
- Pig—oink, oink
- Dog—woof, woof
- Cat—meow, meow
- Hen—cluck, cluck
- Horse—neigh, neigh
- Mouse—squeak
- Mule—hee, haw
- Cow—moo, moo
- Rooster—cock-a-doodle-do

Finale

Use picture books of zoo animals. Make the sounds of these wild animals and see how many your toddler can imitate.

Encore

Use the following rhyme as a guessing game. When you get to the name of an animal, pause and let your toddler fill in those she knows and can say. Repeat the rhyme many times until your toddler knows them all.

"Bow-wow," says the (pause) dog;
"Meow, meow," says the (pause) cat;
"Grunt, grunt," says the (pause) hog;
And "squeak," says the (pause) mouse.

"Who-who," says the (pause) owl;
"Caw, caw," says the (pause) crow;
"Quack, quack," says the (pause) duck;
And what people say, you know.

Is It?

Eggs, butter, bread, cheese
Name it quick, if you please.

Overture

Learning to speak is an extremely complex and difficult task. Forcing a child to talk may cause him to withdraw and slow down his natural language development.

Performance

Play: To help your toddler learn how to recognize and name most common objects, play "Is It?"
What you will need: Familiar objects that your toddler can recognize by name: sock, shoe, bear, ball, cup, block, etc.
How to play: Giving a two-year-old many opportunities to say "no" will lessen the impact of the word. Hold one of the toys and ask, "Is this the teddy bear?" Keep asking if the object you are holding is the thing you named, until the object is correctly identified. Repeat with other objects. If your child has the verbal skills, take turns picking a toy and asking the question.

Finale

Gather cartons and packages that hold eggs, butter, cheese, and bread. Recite the rhyme and then point to one of the packages. Ask, "Is this the butter?" If the food indicated is not the same as the food named, ask your toddler to name the food correctly. Make up rhymes, and play the game with other foods that your toddler can name.
Examples:

Apple, banana, or pickle—dill
Name it quick, if you will.

Cookie, crackers, apple, or pie
Name it quick, tell no lie.

Orange, potato, lemon, or tomato
Name it quick, ready, set, go!

Encore

Do not take a child's negativity personally. It is his way of learning independence. If you accept his "no," he will grow to respect it when you tell him "no." Teach your toddler that when you ask, he has a choice; when you tell, there is no choice—he must obey. Giving him many opportunities to make choices will help your toddler develop independence.

Can You Do It?

Can you do it quick as a wink?
Can you do it before I blink?

Overture

Watch your toddler when she is listening, and often she will tip one ear toward the sound she wants to hear.

Performance

Play: To help your toddler learn to follow a two- or three-component request, play "Can You Do It?"
What you will need: Teddy bear, hat, laundry basket, baby blanket, large cardboard box
How to play: Set the toys and containers on the floor between you and your toddler. Give a two-component request. Repeat as many times as needed. Help your toddler do both steps in the correct order. Play several times as needed until your toddler can perform two-component requests. Each time ask, "Can you do it?"

- Put the hat on the bear. Put the bear in the basket. Can you do it?
- Take the bear out of the basket. Take off the bear's hat. Can you do it?
- Put the bear in the box. Cover the box with the blanket. Can you do it?
- Take the blanket off the bear. Take the bear out of the box. Can you do it?

Finale

Give three-component requests using a new set of toys, including a toy car, dolly, teddy bear, baby bottle, baby blanket, basket, bag, and book. Again, repeat the instructions as many times as your toddler needs to hear them.

- Put the car in the box. Put the dolly in the basket. Put the teddy bear in the bag. Can you do it?
- Feed the dolly with the bottle. Wrap the dolly in the blanket. Put the dolly in the basket. Can you do it?

Encore

Providing experiences that require your toddler to listen is the best way you can teach her how to listen. Play games that will stimulate her listening:

- Shake a glass with ice and ask him to listen to the sound the ice makes against the glass. Have her close her eyes and tell you with a raised hand when she hears the tinkling sound.
- Open a book and shut it with a bang. Say "Open" when you open it and "Shut" when you close it.
- Ring a tiny bell. Tell your toddler to listen for the bell and come to you when she hears you ring it during the day. Several times, ring it and see if she hears it and remembers what to do.
- Line up a glass of ice, a book, and a bell. Have the toddler close her eyes. Then clink the ice, shut the book, or ring the bell. Ask your toddler to tell you which sound she heard by pointing to an object.

Copy Cat

Copy Cat, Copy Cat,
Say what I say.

Overture

When a toddler is learning to speak, it is important for him to hear many spoken words. By modeling a variety of messages, your toddler will begin to formulate an understanding of the words he hears.

Performance

Play: To give your toddler practice speaking in four- to six-word sentences, play "Copy Cat."
What you will need: Easy-to-name toys: book, car, doll, blocks, truck
How to play: Place the objects on the floor between you and your toddler. Pick up one toy and use it in a simple sentence. Use as many one-syllable words as possible. For example: "See the book." Ask the toddler to repeat what you said. "Can you say, 'See the book'?" Demonstrate that you want your toddler to repeat each sentence by repeating them yourself. Repeat the sentence as many times as he needs to hear the words. Talk about each toy in four- to six-word sentences.

- ◆ I see a little car.
- ◆ I like this doll.
- ◆ These are my blocks.
- ◆ This is a truck.

Finale

Use the rhyme and a picture book to play a more advanced version of the game. Sit with your toddler on your lap. Hold the book so he can see the pictures. Open the book, and name something on the first page. You might say: "I see a cat." Point to the cat. Then ask him, "Can you say that? Can you say, 'I see a cat'?" Repeat the four- to six-word sentence slowly, word for word, and then put the words together as a sentence. Demonstrate to your toddler that you want him to say everything you say. Slowly turn the pages of the book, and say one sentence for each page.

Encore

On other occasions, use the rhyme to teach your toddler some interesting names of animals. Use picture books of hard-to-pronounce animals. Together look at the picture of an animal and then say, "Copy Cat, Copy Cat, say what I say—hippopotamus." Sometimes, toddlers enjoy saying big words; make sure you show your child a picture for each word you want him to say.

What's Your Name?

What's your name? Is it Tommy or Sue?
What's your name? May I kiss you?

Overture

The first words for many toddlers are their names and ages. Once a child begins to use a large variety of one-word messages, it is only a matter of a few weeks or months before she can combine these words into sentences.

Performance

Play: To teach your toddler to give her own name and age, play "What's Your Name?"

What you will need: No special equipment is needed to play this game.

How to play: Ask the toddler, "What's your name? Is it Tommy or Sue?" Your toddler might think it is amusing that you are asking her to tell you her name. Ask her several times; each time give the wrong name. Then ask, "What is your name?" Help your toddler learn to say her last name, too. Then teach your toddler that when she is asked how old she is, she may answer "two." She will probably already be able to show two fingers to indicate her age; teach her how to verbalize it, too.

Finale

Use the rhyme and a photograph album of family members to play another version of this game. Look at each photograph, and recite the rhyme. Give your toddler time to respond.
Example:

>What's your name? (*Ask the photograph.*)
>Is it Tommy or Sue? (*Wait for the toddler to shake her head or reply.*)
>What's your name? (*Ask the toddler if she knows the person's name.*)
>May we kiss you? (*Pretend to kiss the person in the photograph.*)

Encore

On other occasions, teach your toddler about meeting strangers. Explain that most people are safe, but some are not. Tell her that she should not be friendly to strangers who ask her name or talk to her when you are not there. Help her distinguish between talking to new people when you are present and avoiding strangers when she is alone or unsupervised. Invent eye signals so she can look to you to find out if it is okay to talk to someone who approaches her. Say something like this: "If a stranger asks you your name, look at me, and I will help you decide if you should talk to that person or not. If I smile and nod that means it is safe, and you can share with the stranger. If I do not think it is safe, I will pick you up and we will leave."

You or Me?

You or me?
We, he, and she?

Overture

Listen to your toddler as he begins to string words together. There will be missing words and sometimes the words will not be in order. Example: "May I eat an apple?" might become, "Me apple eat?" Syntax and grammar are language skills children learn by listening to others.

Performance

Play: To help your toddler learn to understand pronouns: "I," "you," "we," "he," and "she," play "You or Me?"

What you will need: Photograph album of family members

How to play: Sit with your toddler in your lap so he can see the photograph album. Open to the first page. Point to a person and ask, "You, me, he, or she?" You want his response in the form of a pronoun, not a name. If your toddler says, "Daddy," say, "It is *he*. *He* is daddy." Look for photographs of the two of you and say, "There we are. Look what *we* are doing." Point to each photograph soliciting a pronoun. It may be confusing when you say "That is you," because your toddler needs to say, "That is me." And when you say, "That is me," your toddler should say, "That is you." Quiet, patient teaching will help your toddler understand how pronouns are used in place of names.

Finale

Teach possessive pronouns: "his," "hers," and "theirs." Walk around the house pointing to items. Ask, "Whose is this?" Demonstrate that you want a pronoun and not a name. For example: Looking at Brother's bed you might ask, "Whose bed is this?" When your toddler names his brother, say, "This is *his* room." Ask, "Is this *your* bed? No, this is *his* bed." On other occasions, introduce additional pronouns of possession: "yours," "mine," and "ours."

◆ Whose house is this?
◆ Whose mittens are these? Yours or mine?

Encore

Continue the learning outside by taking a walk in your neighborhood. Use pronouns to describe the things you see.

◆ Whose porch is that? (That is *their* porch.)
◆ Whose tree is that? (That is *their* tree.)
◆ Whose truck is that? (That is *his* truck.)
◆ Whose car is that? (That is *her* car.)

One Bear, Two Bears

One bear, two bears.
Three bears, four!

Overture

Listen to your toddler babble to herself. Some speech authorities believe that the key to language acquisition lies in a toddler's babbling. If there is a total lack of external stimuli and the lack of viable contact with a caring adult, a child will not learn to talk because speech is a skill one cannot acquire on one's own.

Performance

Play: To help your toddler begin using plurals correctly ("toys," "balls," etc.), play "One Bear, Two Bears."

What you will need: Pairs of toys that the toddler can name: two stuffed teddy bears, stack of blocks, several books, etc.

How to play: Place the toys on the floor between you and your toddler. Hold up one teddy bear and say "One bear." Hold up two bears and say "Two bears." Put the emphasis on the "s" at the end of "bears" when describing the plural form. Then hold up one bear and ask "What is this?" Listen for the singular "bear." Then hold up two bears and ask, "What are these?" Listen for the plural "bears." Work with one and two bears, then introduce other toys in the same manner. Hold up one block and say, "block." Point to the pile of blocks and say, "blocks." Ask questions to solicit the singular and plural for "blocks." Repeat with books and other toys. If at first your toddler does not seem to understand this process or forgets to use plurals after the game is over, that is only to be expected. The purpose of this game is just to introduce a concept, not master it.

Finale

Use the first line of the rhyme as a guessing game.
> You say, "One bear, two (pause)." (*Toddler is to say the plural "bears."*)
> You say "One book, two (pause)." (*Toddler is to say the plural "books."*)

Walk around the house or yard and recite the line pausing for your toddler to fill in the plural form of the objects you name.
- ◆ One tree, two (pause) trees.
- ◆ One bed, two (pause) beds.
- ◆ One cookie, two (pause) cookies.

Encore

Sometimes, adults forget that irregular speech patterns might completely baffle a toddler. In informal ways, introduce irregular plurals:
- ◆ Foot and feet
- ◆ Deer and deer
- ◆ Mouse and mice
- ◆ Moose and moose

Of course, your toddler does not have to memorize the irregular plural forms. Just introduce them in conversations in an informal way so she will know that there are exceptions to the "add-an-'s'-to-make-a-plural" rule.

Which One?

Red fish, blue fish,
Big fish, little fish.

Overture

Watch your toddler, and you will often see him sorting things by color, shape, and size. Sorting and classifying objects is the way toddlers learn. In the coming months, seeing how things are the same and how they are different is one of the most important skills that your toddler will master.

Performance

Play: To help your toddler begin to use adjectives, play "Which One?"

What you will need: Assortment of toys that are red and blue and big and little such as: red ball, blue ball, large book, small book, red and blue crayons

How to play: Most toddlers cannot name all the colors, but many know red and blue. To play this game, place the toys on the floor between you and your toddler. Ask the toddler to choose something "big." Then say something like this: "Yes, that is a big book." Then take the object and ask, "What is this?" Your toddler may use the adjective when telling you it is a book. Repeat with the other toys. Do not overwhelm your child with more than four adjectives at a time.

Finale

If the toddler knows red from blue, use the rhyme to play a guessing game. Cut four fish shapes from construction paper. They should include:

- ◆ Big red fish
- ◆ Little red fish
- ◆ Big blue fish
- ◆ Little blue fish

The first level of this game is to have your toddler show you the fish you name. For example: "Please show me which one is the big red fish." The second level is for you to pick up a fish and have the toddler tell you about it.

Encore

Food is highly motivating and offers great opportunities for demonstrating a variety of descriptive words. While eating, describe foods such as:

- ◆ Soft (dinner roll, marshmallow, fruit-flavored gelatin)
- ◆ Sticky (peanut butter, honey, jelly)
- ◆ Smooth (milkshake, cream cheese, butter)
- ◆ Cold (ice cream, ice cube, iced juice)
- ◆ Sweet (honey, sugar)

The Itsy, Bitsy Spider

The itsy, bitsy spider went up the water spout.
Down came the rain and washed the spider out.
Out came the sun and dried up all the rain,
And the itsy, bitsy spider went up the spout again.
—Traditional Rhyme

Overture

In order for your toddler to expand her intellectual and creative horizons, you will want to broaden her experiences as much as possible. Playing games with your toddler is a sure way to pique her interest in language.

Performance

Play: To help your toddler use the spatial relationship words "up" and "down," play "The Itsy, Bitsy Spider."

What you will need: Two dots drawn on your knuckles to represent the spider's eyes. Your fingers will be the spider's legs.

How to play: At age two, most toddlers do not identify spatial adverbs. Certainly your toddler's first special adverbs will be "up" and "down." She might say "up" when she wants to be picked up and "down" to be put down. This game is to teach the direction of things moving up or down. Use your hand to have the spider walk *up* a wall and *down* a wall. Use the adverb as your hand ("spider") walks up and down. For example: "See the spider walking *up* the wall. Now the spider is walking *down* the wall." Draw eyes on your toddler's hand and have her use her "spider" to follow commands:

◆ Have your spider walk up your arm. . . . down your arm.
◆ Have your spider walk up the sofa. . . . down the sofa.
◆ Have your spider walk up my arm. . . . down my back.

Finale

Example:
The itsy, bitsy spider went up the water spout.
(*Use fingers of right hand to "walk" up the left arm.*)
Down came the rain and washed the spider out.
(*Wiggle fingers of both hands to represent rain coming down.*)
Out came the sun and dried up all the rain,
(*Open hands and arms in a wide circle in front of your body.*)
And the itsy, bitsy spider went up the spout again.
(*Use fingers of right hand to "walk" up the left arm.*)

Encore

On other occasions, use spatial relationship words while out-of-doors. For example:

◆ Look *up* and see the clouds.
◆ Look *down* and see the ladybug in the grass.
◆ Look *back* and see the car behind our car.

        137

Where Is It?

Where have you been all the day, my boy, Willy?
Where have you been all the day, my boy, Willy? . . .
—Traditional Rhyme

Overture

Naming objects that they can see comes easily for most toddlers. Stringing nouns together into sentences is much more complicated. The more you model speech for your toddler, the more quickly she will learn to speak in sentences.

Performance

Play: To encourage the toddler to use words such as "in," "on," "over," and "under" to describe physical relationships, play "Where Is It?"

What you will need: Teddy bear, stocking cap, basket

How to play: Use the hat and the teddy bear to teach words describing physical relationships.

◆ Place the hat on the bear and ask your toddler, "Where is the hat?" (The hat is *on* the bear.)
◆ Place the bear in the basket and ask the toddler, "Where is the bear?" (The bear is *in* the basket.)
◆ Place the basket over the bear and ask the toddler, "Where is the bear?" (The bear is *under* the basket.)
◆ Place the hat on the bear and ask, "Where is the bear?" (The bear is *under* the hat. The hat is *on* the bear.)

Finale

Use the rhyme to talk with your toddler about places you have been. For example, after returning from the supermarket, recite a personalized version of the rhyme.
Example:
Where have you been all the day,
My boy/girl, (toddler's name)?
Where have you been all the day,
My boy/girl, (toddler's name)?
When talking about where you have been and what you have seen, pay attention to words that show physical relationships. For example, "Remember when we walked *over* the bridge?"

Encore

On other occasions, ask the toddler questions that require a physical relationship answer. For example: "Are your shoes *on* or *under* your bed?" or "Is the milk *in* or *on* the refrigerator?"

Puppets

Tick, tock, tick, tock,
The mouse ran up the clock.

Overture

Children respond to puppet play when they are toddlers more enthusiastically than at any other age. Use puppet play to become a catalyst for creative language development.

Performance

Play: To give the toddler practice repeating nonsense sounds, use puppets.

What you will need: Locate a hand puppet of any kind. The puppet can be an old sock with glued on facial features made of cloth cutouts. Puppets are especially good for language development because toddlers love to talk to puppets and will respond to them as if they were alive.

How to play: Seat your toddler in your lap and put the puppet on your hand. Begin by greeting the toddler with a funny voice that you can save just for the puppet's voice. Ask the toddler questions you know she can answer. Have a conversation with your toddler using the puppet. You may gain some insight when your toddler tells the puppets things that she has never told you. You can also use a puppet to approach scary feelings or hurtful experiences.

Finale

Use the rhyme and a puppet to make the sound of a ticking clock. Have the puppet recite the poem, saying each word in the rhythm of a clock's slow ticking. The puppet can move from side to side like a clock pendulum as you say the rhyme together. Later have the toddler say the first line and the puppet say the last line.
Example:

Tick, tock, tick, tock,
The mouse ran up the clock.

Encore

On other occasions, use the puppet and other nonsense verses to help your toddler learn and say new sounds. Examples:

- ◆ "Gobble, gobble, gobble," said the goose.
- ◆ "V'room, v'room, v'room," went the race car.
- ◆ "Drip, drip, drip," leaked the faucet.
- ◆ "Buzz, buzz, buzz," hummed the bumblebee.
- ◆ "Moo, moo, moo," bellowed mother cow.
- ◆ "Goo, goo, goo," said the tiny baby.

You and your toddler will think of many more interesting sounds to make. Include any sounds that are unique to your toddler when playing this game, too.

Make a Recording

I can sing, I can rhyme,
I can dance in time.

Overture..

A cassette player with a good selection of sing-along or activity tapes will do much to advance your toddler's language skills.

Performance...

Play: To review all the language skills your toddler is acquiring make a special tape recording of his voice.

What you will need: Tape recorder

How to play: Encourage your toddler to sing favorite songs, recite favorite rhymes, or tell stories. Whatever new words he has acquired this year, record them for posterity. After creating the tape, listen to it together. Tell your toddler how pleased and proud you are that he can communicate with you. Listen to the tape with family members. In fact, make several tapes to send to relatives who live in other states. Keep one tape and date it with your toddler's exact age. Put it in a safe place. Someday it will be among your most valued treasures.

Finale...

Use the rhymes and finger plays learned in this chapter to make tapes. You can tape yourself singing favorite songs or lullabies so your toddler can hear your voice when you are away on a trip or simply gone for the day.

Encore..

On other occasions, make a video of your toddler doing all the new things he has learned to do this year. Watch the video together. Talk about all of the wonderful things your toddler is learning to do. Praise his every effort. Include some of these:

- Walking
- Galloping
- Dancing
- Painting
- Drawing with a pencil
- Drinking from a cup
- Putting together a puzzle
- Riding a pedal toy
- Playing with a dolly
- Climbing
- Opening a door
- Putting on socks
- Hopping
- Standing on tiptoes
- Making music
- Coloring with crayons
- Using play clay
- Eating with a spoon
- Pulling a toy
- Wearing dress-up clothes
- Rocking a teddy bear
- Walking up stairs
- Bouncing a ball
- Brushing teeth

Keeping Track

Milestone	Date	Comments
Can mimic most sounds heard		
Responds verbally to things around him/her		
Can sing simple songs		
Can make sounds of some animals		
Recognizes and names most common objects		
Can obey a two- or three-component request		
Can speak in four- to six-word sentences		
Can give own name and age		
Uses pronouns: "I," "you," "we," "she"		
Uses plurals correctly: "toys," "balls," etc.		
Uses some adjectives: "red," "blue," "big," "little"		
Uses spatial relationships: "up" and "down"		
Uses spatial relationships: "in," "on," "over," and "under"		
Can repeat nonsense sounds		

One, Two, Red, Blue

Cognitive/Creative Development

 Contemplate

In their third year, toddlers celebrate a rapid development of reasoning capabilities. As youngsters acquire language, they can form mental images for things, actions, and concepts. They can solve problems by thinking instead of experimenting. During this developmental stage, your toddler will begin stringing together a series of actions that produce logical results. As his knowledge of cause and effect develops, he will be interested in play that results in predictable outcomes. For example, winding a music box results in music.

Toddlers have rich imaginations; they do not need props to play games. Holding his hand to his ear may mean talking on a telephone, or pretending to turn a stirring wheel may be the child's way of driving a make-believe car. Encourage your toddler to be creative by sometimes having him play without toys. Be patient with your child's intellectual growth. Do not try to rush him. Just as we cannot open a cocoon to set a butterfly free or remove the outer petals to rush the blooming of a rose, we cannot speed up a child's cognitive development. Just as the universe is whirling through space at exactly the right speed, your toddler is developing at his own perfect pace. Use the games in this chapter to practice the milestones listed below.

Cognitive/Creative Milestones: 24 to 36 months

- ◆ Will learn that things out-of-sight still exist
- ◆ Will learn to sit still long enough to hear a story
- ◆ Will learn that pictures represent real objects (and can match)
- ◆ Will learn to work mechanical toys
- ◆ Will learn to play make-believe with dolls and stuffed animals
- ◆ Will learn to sort objects by color, size, or shape
- ◆ Will learn how some objects are part of a whole (puzzle pieces)
- ◆ Will learn the concepts of one/more than one
- ◆ Will learn that certain actions result in specific outcomes
- ◆ Will learn that some things are predictable (Father/Mother leaves and then comes home at certain times each day.)
- ◆ Will learn to make musical sounds
- ◆ Will be able to make associations between familiar objects and the people to whom they belong
- ◆ Will become increasingly aware of nature around him
- ◆ Will enjoy experimenting to discover how things fit together
- ◆ Will enjoy experimenting to discover what is inside things

General Tips

Have faith in your toddler's ability to learn. She is smart. Her intelligence is incredible! Be patient with your child's cognitive progress. Do not let learning plateaus worry you. Some days it may even seem that she is regressing. That is as it should be. Learning does not travel on a straight-forward path. You can enhance your child's growing environment, but you cannot accelerate the force from within that makes her grow.

Removing something from a child's sight will no longer end her desire to have it, as it did when she was an infant. If you take something from your child and put it away, she will remember where it is and may insist on having it even though she cannot see it. That is because she has learned an important concept called "permanency"—things exist even when they are not visible.

Many two-year-olds are *eager helpers*. They like to perform tasks that are valued in the adult world. Letting your toddler help around the house is not only good practice for fine motor and gross motor skills, but it will also give your toddler great self-satisfaction. Appropriate chores for a two-year-old include:

- ◆ Washing and tearing large lettuce leaves for a salad
- ◆ Scrubbing vegetables with a brush
- ◆ Cutting cookies with a cookie cutter
- ◆ Stirring cake batter with a spoon
- ◆ Placing letters in the mailbox
- ◆ Sorting socks by colors
- ◆ Clearing the dinner table of unbreakable items
- ◆ Watering plants with a small watering can
- ◆ Folding small kitchen towels
- ◆ Picking up her own toys
- ◆ Dusting furniture
- ◆ Sweeping the floor with a child-sized broom

When playing learning games with your toddler, do not tell her if she is doing something wrong or show her how to do it "better." Instead, let your toddler discover the answers for herself. Be flexible in what is required. The object is to learn—any amount of new knowledge is excellent progress. If an activity seems too difficult and is frustrating for your toddler, save it for another day when she is older and has learned additional skills. Every day your toddler will make giant intellectual leaps, but intellectual skills may be more difficult to see and appreciate than motor skills.

Praise her every new accomplishment. Remember, if she thinks she can or if she thinks she cannot accomplish a task, she will live up to her own expectations.

Cognitive/Creative Development 24- to 36-Month-Old

(See above.)

© Instructional Fair • TS Denison

143

Hide-and-Seek

There was an old woman who lived under a hill,
And if she's not gone, she lives there still.

Overture

By the time a toddler is two years of age the size of his brain has reached 90% of an adult's size brain. Since the brain continues its maturation and refinement during the preschool years, there is still a great deal of neurological development going on.

Performance

Play: To help your toddler visualize things that he cannot see play "Hide-and-Seek."

What you will need: Large, colorful toy such as a stuffed animal

How to play: Have the toddler close his eyes while you hide the toy in the room. Leave a bit of the toy exposed. With eyes open but remaining in place, your toddler is to look around the room until he spots the toy. When the toy has been spotted, let your toddler retrieve it. Then, if it is appropriate for your child's language ability, have him tell you where the toy was hidden. Examples: "Bear was on the television," "Bear was behind the sofa," or "Bear was under the table." If your child cannot tell you where the toy was hidden, verbalize for him. Say, "I hid the teddy bear under the sofa cushion." Take turns hiding and finding the toy.

Finale

To play this game, you will need three small identical boxes without lids and a small toy that will fit under the boxes. As your child watches, place the toy under one of the three boxes. Shuffle the boxes. Recite the rhyme, and then let your toddler point to the box under which he thinks the toy is hidden. Let him lift the boxes while searching for the toy. When he finds the toy, talk about where it was hidden. "The car was *under* this box."

Encore

On other occasions, help your toddler visualize where things are located. For example, when preparing to brush teeth, ask: "Where is the toothpaste?" Allow time for the toddler to point to the drawer where the toothpaste is kept. If his response is correct, verbally praise him. If his response is incorrect, say something like this: "That was a very excellent guess." Then point to the place where the toothpaste is actually kept and say, "Let's look in here and see if we can find it."

Story Time

One, two, time for a nap;
Three, four, sit in my lap.

Overture

Watch and you will see that your toddler is interested in age-appropriate books. Books that are not age-appropriate will not hold her interest.

Performance

Play: To help your toddler learn how to sit still long enough to hear a story, read to your toddler every day.

What you will need: Picture books

How to play: Read beautifully illustrated books to your toddler every day. Sit with your child in your lap and show her how to turn the pages. Read for just as long as she can sit quietly in your lap. Remember, learning to listen and sit silently is a skill that takes a great deal of time to master. Use the rhyme to signal that you are about to open to the first page of a book. Recited softly, the verse can be a reminder that you are waiting and will open the book when she is still and listening. Owning her own books is also a good way to teach an early appreciation for books. Visit your local library, and if they have a story time for toddlers, enroll her in the program.

Finale

When choosing books for your two-year-old, include books with:
- Bright, distinctive, attractive illustrations
- Illustrations that are repeated on several pages
- Illustrations that invite sound effects
- Illustrations that encourage participation
- Stories about "calamities"
- Pages that can be manipulated (touch-and-feel or tabs to lift)
- Easy-to-turn sturdy pages

Encore

Make sure your toddler has cardboard books especially designed for two-year-olds. Appropriate books for toddlers include:
- *Goodnight Moon* by Margaret Wise Brown (HarperCollins Juvenile Books, 1991)
- *Guess How Much I Love You* by Sam McBratney (Candlewick Press, 1996)
- *The Runaway Bunny* by Margaret Wise Brown (HarperCollins Juvenile Books, 1972)
- *Mr. Brown Can Moo! Can You?* by Dr. Seuss (Random House, 1991)
- *Snoozers: 7 Short Bedtime Stories for Lively Little Kids* by Sandra Boynton (Little Simon, 1997)
- *Sheep in a Jeep* by Nancy Shaw (Houghton Mifflin Co., 1997). Also keep in mind: *Sheep in a Shop, Sheep on a Ship,* and *Sheep Out to Eat,* all by the same author, Nancy Shaw.
- *Jamberry* by Bruce Degen (Harperfestival, 1995)

Can We Find It?

Little Bo Peep has lost her sheep,
And can't tell where to find them. . . .
—Traditional Rhyme

Overture

Between the ages of two and three, toddlers grasp that symbols represent real things. A picture of a puppy in a book is not a puppy, but it represents a puppy. This understanding that real objects have symbols, which may be pictures or written words, is the first step in learning to read.

Performance

Play: To help your toddler learn how to "read" pictures, play "Can We Find It?"
What you will need: Picture book with farm animals and stuffed or plastic farm animals, such as a lamb, pig, dog, or cat
How to play: Sit with the toddler in your lap. Look at a stuffed animal, for example, a lamb. Name it, saying, "This is a lamb." Then ask, "Can we find a picture of a lamb?" Look in the picture book at the animals and find the lamb. Ask questions as you are looking at each animal picture in the book. "Look. Is this a lamb? No, it is a cow. Can we find a lamb?" Repeat with animal pictures until you find the picture of a lamb. Share only a few animal matches in one sitting.

Finale

Use variations of the rhyme to have your toddler find named animals in a pile of toys. Using the same four stuffed or plastic animals above, recite the verse.
Example:

> Little (toddler's name)
> Has lost her lamb (pig, dog, cat),
> And can't tell where to find it.

See if your toddler can pick out from the pile the animal you have named. Repeat with each of the animals in the pile.

Encore

On other occasions, use a personalized version of the rhyme to find objects in a pile of five or six things. Recite the verse and let your toddler find the named object.
Example:

> Little (toddler's name)
> Has lost his *ball*,
> And can't tell where to find it.

Jack-in-the-Box

Round and round the mulberry bush, the monkey chased the weasel,
The monkey stopped, the weasel stopped.
Pop! Goes the weasel.
—Traditional Song

Overture

Automobiles and mechanical objects hold great fascination for toddlers. From an early age, most children want to operate machines. Watch a toddler get behind the wheel in a car, and she will probably grab the steering wheel and turn it. Being able to turn a crank, flip a switch, or push a handle and make something move, gives toddlers a feeling of great power.

Performance

Play: To help your toddler learn how to work mechanical toys, play with a "Jack-in-the-Box."
What you will need: Jack-in-the-box wind-up toy
How to play: Sit on the floor with your toddler. Place the jack-in-the-box on the floor between you and your toddler. Turn the crank and sing the appropriate song or hum along. (Many jack-in-the-boxes use "Pop! Goes the Weasel.") When you get to the point just before "Jack" pops up, pause and look at your toddler. Let the suspense build. Then continue winding so the "Jack" pops up. Push "Jack" back down and close the lid. Repeat, letting your toddler turn the crank. If she needs help, guide her hand with yours. Pause just before "Jack" pops up again.

Finale

Use this version to play an action game.
Example:
    Round and round the mulberry bush, (*Chase toddler around in a circle.*)
    The monkey chased the weasel, (*Keep moving in a circle.*)
    The monkey stopped, the weasel stopped. (*Stop and sit down. Toddler is to sit down, too.*)
    Pop! Goes the weasel. (*Jump up and chase her again.*)

Try a personalized version of rhyme too.
    Round and round the mulberry bush, (*Chase the toddler around in a circle.*)
    Mommy chased (toddler's name), (*Keep moving in a circle.*)
    Mommy stopped, (toddler's name) stopped. (*Stop and sit down.*)
    Pop! Goes the people. (*Jump up and chase her again.*)

Encore

Provide a variety of exploration and mastery play materials for the toddler including:
- Hidden-object pop-up boxes (with lids, doors, dials, switches, knobs)
- Simple lock boxes
- Shape sorters with common shapes
- Tool chests with plastic tools and a plastic tool bench

Feed the Baby

Open wide.
Feed the baby.

Overture..

For most toddlers, the greatest inducement for pretending is to play with an adult or older child who enjoys the game, too.

Performance..

Play: To encourage the toddler to play make-believe with dolls and stuffed animals, play "Feed the Baby."

What you will need: Dolls and teddy bears, plastic bowl and spoon, dry cereal or raisins

How to play: Pour some dry cereal in the bowl. Show your toddler how to use the spoon to scoop up the cereal and pretend to feed the doll. Say, "Open wide. Feed the baby." Pretend to feed the bears and other stuffed toys, too. Your toddler can eat the cereal or put it back in the bowl after pretending to feed the dolls and bears.

Finale..

Encourage your toddler to play with the doll as if it was a baby. Include these activities:
- ◆ Bathe the doll in a small tub of water and dry it with a towel.
- ◆ Wrap the doll in a blanket, feed it, burp it, and rock it.
- ◆ Dress and undress the doll.
- ◆ Push the doll in a toy carriage.
- ◆ Carry the doll around in a careful way.
- ◆ Rock the doll and put it to bed.

Encore...

On other occasions, use a refrigerator-sized box to make a play place. Turn it upside down so the bottom of the box is on the top. Create a slanted roof by opening the top flaps halfway and duct taping the edges together to form a triangle. Cut out big windows and a door. Encourage your toddler to play inside with dolls and stuffed toys. The box can become a playhouse, a store, a castle, a puppet theater, a fort, or anything else on which the toddler might decide. A nondescript box is a good play place because it is not limited by designs painted on the outside. Your toddler's rich imagination will turn it into whatever kind of place he wants in which to play.

Which Is Different?

Polly put on the spoons and knives,
Susy put on the plates and forks.

Overture

Teaching your toddler that things can be sorted according to attributes is an important step in her intellectual development.

Performance

Play: To help your toddler learn how to sort objects by color, size, or shape, play "Which Is Different?"

What you will need: Plastic and paper picnic supplies: knives, spoons, forks, plates, bowls, cups (three each); picnic blanket; basket

How to play: Lay out the picnic blanket to indicate the picnic spot. Set the basket of supplies on the blanket between you and your toddler. Place two spoons and one cup in a row. Ask, "Which one is different?" "Different" may be a new concept, so show the toddler that the cup is "not the same" as the spoons. Then put the cup back in the basket. Set the plate next to the spoons. Ask, "Is this the same as the spoons?" Continue until you have a match of three spoons. Repeat the game using two plates and a fork. Have your toddler pick up the one that is not a match and put it back into the basket. After your toddler understands the game, encourage her to find the third matching item for the pair you have set out on the blanket. Continue the matching game in an informal way. Let your toddler put two items out for you to match, etc.

Finale

Use clothing to play this game, including: (three each of unmatched) shoes, socks, ties, scarves, mittens, etc. Have the toddler find the three that are alike. In using alike, but not matching items, the toddler is challenged to determine in what way the objects are alike. For example: all are shoes or all are scarves.

Encore

On other occasions, cut paper shapes as follows:
- ◆ Three large red squares
- ◆ Three large blue squares
- ◆ Three large yellow squares
- ◆ Three large red circles
- ◆ Three large blue circles
- ◆ Three large yellow circles

Place two matching shapes of the same color on the table. For example: Two red squares. Let the toddler look at the other cutouts to find the third one that is the same color *and* shape. Have your toddler place the matching cutout on the table next to the pair. If this is too difficult, begin with just red and blue squares. On another day use three different colors of squares. As the toddler learns how to play the game, introduce the circles.

Puzzles

Riddle me, riddle me, ree,
Put this puzzle together with me.

Overture..

Watch your toddler playing with a puzzle, and you will see his patience at work. Putting together puzzles takes strategy. Once the toddler learns the strategy, he will lose interest in that particular puzzle.

Performance..

Play: To help your toddler learn how some objects are part of a whole, begin with puzzles having four to eight pieces.

What you will need: Puzzles

How to play: When introducing your toddler to a new puzzle, place the puzzle on the floor or table between you and your toddler. Look at the puzzle with all of the pieces in place. Talk about the picture or object of the puzzle. Remove one piece and examine how the puzzle looks without that piece. Put the piece back into the puzzle and remove another piece. Look and discuss how the puzzle looks without that piece. Have your toddler put the piece back in the puzzle. Repeat this process examining the puzzle with each piece removed. Then remove two puzzle pieces. Each time, let your toddler put the puzzle pieces back in the puzzle. When the puzzle is back together, let your toddler take out a piece and put it back. Eventually, he will want to take out all the pieces and put the whole thing back together again.

Finale..

Create puzzles with pictures cut from magazines. First, reinforce the picture by attaching it to heavy paper. Then cut the picture in half. The cut should be straight across, horizontally or vertically, so the toddler only needs to line them up correctly. Help your toddler put the homemade puzzles together, then let him try to match the pieces for his first puzzle experience. Use photocopies of photographs of your toddler, family members, and favorite objects to make personalized puzzles, too.

Encore..

Remember, all beginning puzzles should be big, bright, and simple for your toddler to do. Start with two- or three-piece puzzles and as the toddler learns to do these, promote him to puzzles with five or six pieces. Include wooden puzzles that have little knobs. Wooden puzzles with knobs give your toddler an opportunity to use fine motor skills and eye-hand coordination. Some more complicated puzzles are also created especially for toddlers and require more strategy. It will delight your toddler if you work with him until he understands the object of each new puzzle.

How Many?

One is lonely,
Some is company.
Many is a crowd.

Overture

The first number a toddler usually learns is "two" because that is how old she is. Toddlers do not need to learn to count or comprehend which numerals stand for specific amounts. Teaching your toddler that numbers represent certain amounts is sufficient.

Performance

Play: To help your toddler learn the concept of more than one ("two" or "three") and too many to count, play "How Many?"

What you will need: Pile of blocks

How to play: There are ways to tell "how many" without counting. Toddlers are not ready to count, but they can distinguish between "one," "some," and "many." Place blocks on the floor between you and your toddler. Pick up one block and say, "One. This is *one* block." Pick up three or four blocks and say, "Here are *some* blocks." Then indicate the whole pile of blocks and say, "These are *many* blocks." Next use blocks to represent one of the three: "one," "some," or "many." Ask, "How many?" Do them quickly and in random order. Make a fun guessing game of the questions and answers. Then have the toddler challenge you by presenting "one," "some," or "many" blocks and you must tell her how many.

Finale

Walk around your house or yard and look for things that are single, double, or in large numbers. Talk about them.

- There are *many* apples on the tree.
- There are *some* cars on the street.
- There is *one* porch on our house.

While driving in the car, ask questions that can be answered with "one," "some," or "many."

- How many people do you see?
- How many trees do you see?
- How many houses do you see?

Encore

On other occasions, use a small wagon and a pile of blocks to play "Bring Me." Place the blocks at the opposite end of the room. Tell your toddler to bring "one," "some," or "many" blocks. Then, she must pull the wagon to the pile of blocks, remember what you asked for and put that number in the wagon, and pull it back to you. Verbalize the amount of blocks in the wagon. "Thank you for bringing me *some* blocks." Then ask her to bring you another amount of blocks. Repeat.

Watch the Big Bouncing Ball

Bounce and fall, bounce and fall,
Watch the big bouncing ball.

Overture

Many toys can be played with alone, but a ball is the toy that plays better when shared with a playmate.

Performance

Play: To help your toddler learn that certain actions result in specific outcomes, play "Watch the Big Bouncing Ball."

What you will need: Big rubber ball

How to play: Demonstrate through play that the same thing always happens when you use a ball in certain ways:

- ◆ When a ball is dropped, it bounces.
- ◆ When a ball is thrown up, it comes back down.

Toss the ball in the air. On the way up say, "up." As the ball is falling say, "down." Play for awhile, tossing the ball up and verbalizing its direction. Then bounce the ball and do the same thing. As the ball is in the fall, say, "down." When it bounces, say, "up." Verbalize the direction of the ball for both of the actions: tossing and bouncing.

Finale

After your toddler understands that tossed balls fall back and dropped balls bounce, introduce the concept of "rolling." Through play, demonstrate that:

- ◆ When a ball is rolled, it does not come back.
- ◆ When a ball is rolled against something, it does come back.

Roll the ball out into the room where it will not hit anything. When it stops moving, say, "stops." Roll the ball toward a wall, and when it reverses direction, say, "comes back." Play rolling ball games and verbalize what is happening to the ball.

Encore

On other occasions, talk about other predictable outcomes. Signal your toddler before you do something that will cause something predictable to happen including:

- ◆ Flip the light switch—It gets dark.
- ◆ Touch the garage door opener—The garage door goes up or down.
- ◆ Turn off the television—There is no picture or sound.
- ◆ Turn on the water faucet—Water gushes out.
- ◆ Turn the key in the ignition of the car—The engine starts.
- ◆ Blow into a horn—There is a sound.
- ◆ Put powdered chocolate mix in milk—It turns brown and chocolate.
- ◆ Put cookies in a hot oven—They bake.

Playhouse

Bye, baby, bunting, Daddy's gone a-hunting,
To get a little rabbit skin to wrap his baby bunting in.
—Traditional Rhyme

Overture

Most toddlers enjoy playing in playhouses; farms or with miniature replications of houses (for dolls), farms, toy villages with tiny plastic people, miniature railroads, and garages with small cars, trucks, and airplanes. However, toys that are replications of the real world will not be enjoyed by toddlers who have not experienced the real world.

Performance

Play: To help your toddler learn that some things are predictable (Father/Mother leaves and then comes home at certain times each day), play with miniature plastic people and a tiny playhouse.
What you will need: Plastic play-scene materials such as people, a few vehicles, and a little playhouse the right size for the people
How to play: Informally, use the people and house to play. Designate a toy to be each member of your family. Families come in many shapes, so be representative of your family in this play. As the "daddy" leaves to go to work, have family members tell him good-bye, kiss, etc. Use a little car for the father to drive off to work. Mother can leave for work, too, if that represents your family's circumstances. Create dialogues with the miniature people. Listen to discover your toddler's concerns and interests regarding specific family members. Follow your toddler's lead.

Finale

Playhouses big enough for the toddler to get inside are very popular toys at this age. Older toddlers like to pretend to be the mother, the father, the baby, or an older sibling and enjoy playing house. They can also change roles during their play. By this age, children are better able to imagine objects and can begin to create extra props for pretend play. They may use blocks or other objects, such as a piece of cloth for a blanket or a dress-up cape. Playhouse props can include: dolls, furniture (play stove, sink, cupboard), shopping cart, cooking equipment (pots and pans with lids), safe eating utensils, empty plastic food containers, and so on.

Encore

On other occasions, encourage your toddler to use dress-up clothes that belong to family members to play house. A box or chest where clothes will be easily accessible is best. In free play, the toddler can choose Father's shirt or Mother's blouse to play a role. Safe, flat shoes that your toddler can slip on over her own shoes are usually enjoyed by children this age. Hats, belts, and scarves make good dress-up accessories, too.

Make Music

Here we go up, up, up, and here we go down, down, downy.
Here we go backward and forward, and here we go round, round, round.
—Traditional Rhyme

Overture

For toddlers, moving to music is a release of their natural sense of rhythm. Although most toddlers are not yet very sophisticated about music, most enjoy rhythms and can keep time with a beat.

Performance

Play: To encourage your toddler to make musical sounds, play "Make Music."

What you will need: Objects that can be used to make interesting sounds include:

- Keys on a ring to jingle
- Pots and pans to beat with wooden spoons
- Pan lids to bang together
- Empty oatmeal carton to pound like a drum
- Bells to ring

How to play: Provide a box of objects that can be used to make "music." Encourage your toddler to play with the objects however he chooses. Praise your toddler for the "music" he makes. Make music together.

Finale

Recite the rhyme, play musical instruments, and parade around the room. Use a marching step, and keep time to the music. In the beginning, lead the parade. Later, let your toddler lead the parade and set the tempo of the march. As your toddler becomes familiar with the verse, move in the directions indicated by marching forward on the first line and backward on the second line. Change from backward to forward on the third line, and march in a circle on the last line.

Encore

Two-year-olds respond enthusiastically to musical and rhythm instruments. Since their fine motor coordination and finger dexterity are improving, they can handle drums, tambourines, sand blocks, triangles, and rhythm sticks. Musical instrument sets can be purchased that include a variety of instruments appropriate for toddlers. Music should be an important part of your toddler's day, and the more opportunity he has to make his own music the better.

Whose Shoes?

Shoe the horse, and shoe the mare,
But let the little colt go bare.
—Traditional Rhyme

Overture

A question that children discover between the ages of two and three is "Whose?" Toddlers learn quickly what belongs to them. "Mine" is often one of their favorite words. However, for toddlers, the other side of the coin—honoring other people's possessions—is a bit more complicated.

Performance

Play: To help your toddler make associations between familiar objects and the people to whom they belong, play "Whose Shoes?"

What you will need: Collect a variety of shoes from members of the family. If your family is small, borrow shoes (rubber boots, slippers, etc.) from Grandma, Grandpa, cousins, etc. If you are using shoes that can be washed in the washing machine, it is a good idea to clean them before playing the game.

How to play: Line up several pairs of shoes. Encourage your toddler to look at the shoes. Then point to a shoe and ask, "Whose shoe?" If your child cannot verbalize the answer, you might direct her by saying, "Point to Grandma's shoes." or "Point to Daddy's shoes." Tell stories about places the shoe owners may have worn the shoes. Example: "These are the boots that Daddy wears when he goes fishing." or "These are the shoes Brother wears when he plays baseball."

Finale

Using a laundry basket of socks, have your toddler help you match socks by colors and sizes. The number of socks to be matched will depend upon the developmental level of your toddler. When you are finished sorting the socks, select a pair and ask, "Whose socks are these? Do they belong to (name of person)?"

Encore

On other occasions, match other pairs of things.
- ◆ Match mittens. (Place four pairs of mittens in a basket and have your toddler find the pairs.)
- ◆ Match colors. (Draw three large spots of color on white paper. Have toddler match three crayons to the same color spots.)

Bird Watching

Little Robin Red-breast sat upon a hurdle,
With a pair of speckled legs and a green girdle.
—Traditional Rhyme

Overture..........

The zest for exploration is heightened when your toddler is exposed to nature. Outings will provide your toddler with all kinds of things to see and discuss. When weather permits, spend time outside with your toddler every single day.

Performance..........

Play: To encourage your toddler to be aware of nature, go bird watching.

What you will need: Any warm day

How to play: Toddlers are usually interested in many things, especially things happening outside. Spend time outside watching the birds. Find a comfortable place where you can both sit quietly. Point out the many different kinds of birds. Watch the birds flying; watch them landing. Feed bread to some birds. How many different sizes of birds can you spot? Enjoy the time you spend bird watching with your toddler.

Finale..........

Take a trip to a pond where your toddler can feed ducks. Watching baby ducks waddling behind their mother can be very entertaining. Ask your toddler questions about the ducks.

- ◆ Which one do you think is the mother?
- ◆ Which ones do you think are the babies?
- ◆ What do the ducks eat?
- ◆ What sounds do the ducks make?

Encore..........

Celebrate each new season with an appropriate outing:

- ◆ In the winter, look for icicles, build a snowperson, lie in the snow and make a snow angel, tromp through the snow, or have a snowball fight.
- ◆ In the summer, look for blooming flowers, ladybugs, and frogs.
- ◆ In the autumn, rake colorful leaves, find a cobweb, star gaze, and gather pinecones.
- ◆ In the spring, look for wildflowers, birds' nests, ant hills, and budding leaves.

Take walks in early morning dew, late afternoon hikes in a park, or walk after dark to gaze up at the stars. Celebrate full moons and sunsets. Pointing out the tremendous beauty in nature will establish a lifelong pattern of appreciation for your toddler—one of the greatest gifts that you will ever give him.

Stack the Boxes

Big box on the bottom,
Middle-sized in the middle,
And a little box on top.

Overture ....

No other non-toy objects hold quite the fascination for toddlers as do cardboard boxes. Cardboard boxes can be used to fill and empty; crawl into, onto, around, and under; and can be stacked into towers.

Performance ....

Play: To encourage the toddler to experiment and discover how things fit together, play "Stack the Boxes."
What you will need: Three or four various-sized boxes with lids
How to play: Demonstrate to the toddler how to build a tower by using the biggest box on the bottom and stacking up to the smallest box on top. Then have her knock the tower down. Help your toddler build the tower again. Soon she will be stacking the boxes and building towers on her own.

Finale ....

Use the rhyme to narrate the building of the tower. Experiment to see what happens:
- ◆ If the little box is placed on top of the big box.
- ◆ If the big box is placed on top of the middle-sized box.
- ◆ If the big box is placed on top of the little box.

Add more boxes of various sizes to the game. Include large cardboard boxes for the base and tiny match boxes for the top of the tower. Work with six or seven boxes. What is the highest tower your toddler can build? Make a little paper flag with a drinking straw pole, and fly it from the top of the tower.

Encore ....

On other occasions, use toys specially designed for stacking. Five- to ten-piece plastic, nesting and stacking toys are fun and educational. One-turn-to-screw-on, barrel nesting toys are also appropriate for this age group. You can make a nesting game with three or four boxes that will fit inside each other. There should be a big difference in sizes so there is plenty of room for nesting. Show the toddler what she can do with them, and let her experiement. Gradually increase the number of boxes as she becomes proficient at nesting them.

What's Inside?

Cut the apple, and what do I see?
A star looking back at me.

Overture

Toddlers are awed by everything they see. Remember, for toddlers everything is new and exciting. One of the greatest gifts your child will give to you is a new way of seeing the world through his eyes.

Performance

Play: To encourage the toddler to wonder about what is inside things, play "What's Inside?"
What you will need: An apple, orange, and banana; small sharp knife; cutting board
How to play: Place the fruit on the cutting board between you and your toddler. Hold up the apple and ask, "What's inside?" Or say, "Will the inside be the same as the outside?" Use the knife to cut the apple in half horizontally. Point out the star-shape created by the seeds. Talk about what is inside the apple. Look at how thick the peel is. Core a piece of apple and encourage him to smell and taste it.

Look at the orange. Ask, "What is inside?" "Will the seeds make a star-shape when we look inside?" Cut the orange in half horizontally. Look at the inside of the fruit. Talk about the aroma and seeds. Taste the orange.

Peel the banana and cut it lengthwise. Look at the tiny seeds. Discuss how the inside of a banana looks. Have your toddler close his eyes and give him a bit of one of the fruits. Have him guess which one it is. Can he tell by smelling a piece of fruit which fruit it is?

Finale

Investigate the inside of other things. Cut the food item in half and discuss:
- ◆ Cookie—Look for identifiable parts.
- ◆ Potato, tomato, and carrot—Look for seeds. Which one has seeds?

Encore

On other occasions, investigate the inside of household appliances to see how they look:
- ◆ Washing machine/dryer
- ◆ Oven
- ◆ Refrigerator/freezer
- ◆ Dishwasher

Talk about how the appliances look inside. This is a good time to warn your toddler of the dangers of climbing inside appliances and discuss safety rules.

Keeping Track

Milestone	Date	Comments
Understands that things out-of-sight exist		
Can sit still to hear a story		
Understands that pictures represent objects		
Can work mechanical toys		
Plays make-believe dolls/stuffed toys		
Can sort objects by color, size, or shape		
Understands some objects are part of a whole		
Understands concepts: "one," "some," "many"		
Understands that actions can result in specific outcomes		
Understands that some things are predictable		
Can make musical sounds		
Can make associations between objects/owners		
Is aware of nature around him/her		
Experiments to discover how things fit together		
Experiments to discover what is inside things		

"Please" and "Thank You"

Social/Emotional Development

Contemplate

When considering your toddler's social development, remember:
- ◆ Two-year-olds need at least one or two regular playmates.
- ◆ Toddlers learn more social skills from other children than they do from their parents.
- ◆ Peer groups offer toddlers rich opportunities to learn social skills: cooperation, sharing, and communicating.

When considering your toddler's emotional development, keep in mind that two-year-olds need a great deal of approval. Do not let your toddler hear you talking about "the terrible two's" or it may be a self-fulfilling prophesy. Whether this developmental stage is *terrible* or *terrific* will depend on how those around your toddler view him. Your toddler is *terrific* and doing exactly what he should be doing at this age. Although society sometimes views a two-year-old's behavior as *terrible*, the two-year-old is simply establishing his independence. Support and praise your toddler's struggle to establish autonomy.

Two-year-olds need to have their feelings validated. When two-year-olds are allowed to experience and express all of their normal impulses such as anger, defiance, aggression, and jealousy, they can grow to be people who are in touch with their true feelings. If, on the other hand, they are required to suppress or deny these feelings, they will not learn to deal with them in appropriate ways. Buried deep within, hurtful feelings may cause a great deal of internal turmoil. Later the feelings may surface in inappropriate ways, such as uncontrollable anger or intense rage. Use the games in this chapter to help your toddler in making friends and finding socially acceptable ways of expressing his true feelings.

Social/Emotional Milestones: 24 to 36 Months
- ◆ Will be enriched by outings and field trips
- ◆ Will begin to enjoy watching television programs
- ◆ Will show preferences and begin to make choices
- ◆ Will begin to understand that other people have rights, too
- ◆ Will begin to enjoy family rituals
- ◆ Will begin to learn social skills by watching peers
- ◆ May begin to practice social skills such as "sharing" and "taking turns"
- ◆ Will experience negative feelings and need ways to release them
- ◆ Will experience joy and need ways to express his happiness
- ◆ Will begin to need ways to relax and release tension
- ◆ Will begin learning self-care skills
- ◆ Will begin to enjoy helping with baking activities
- ◆ Will begin to know the difference between boys and girls
- ◆ Will begin to appreciate and celebrate his own growth and learning

 ## General Tips

For emotional and social growth, *all youngsters need praise and acceptance.* Never underestimate the power of expectations as a force in your toddler's development. Toddlers have an uncanny ability to live up to expectations. If you describe her as "cooperative," "intelligent," "happy," and "safe," she will try to live up to those expectations. On the other hand, if others are negative and tell her that she is "uncooperative," "noisy," "rambunctious," and "accident prone," she may become all those things. *Words are powerful!* If you teach your child to expect miracles, that the world is a good place, and that she is capable of anything, you are giving her the best possible chance of achieving a fulfilled life.

Toddlers also *need to be around other toddlers.* It is not too early to begin teaching your toddler how to play cooperatively with other children. When toddlers first meet, they do not know appropriate ways in which to behave. Hitting may be one child's way of greeting another child. Patiently explain each time when your child is aggressive, that the other child has feelings, too. Show her how to greet peers in a respectful and loving way. When children are given the opportunity to play together, they have the perfect setting to practice social skills. These playtimes will form the foundation for all of your toddler's future interactions. As she encounters new information and experiences, she will establish a strong belief system about how the world works and what people are like. Make sure she has time with other toddlers so she can experience early kinships and celebrate human relationships with peers.

Affection and love are the most important tools you can use to teach a two-year-old. Toddlers act on impulse and often cannot make a distinction between appropriate and inappropriate behavior. Kind words and praise will keep her on the correct path. Remember, examples shape a child's behavior more than any spoken words or sets of rules.

Field Trips

As I was going along, long, long,
I sang a funny song, song, song.

Overture

Exploring the world outside your home will give you a chance to warn your child of dangers, introduce new ideas, and find brand-new things to see, do, and discuss.

Performance

Play: To expand your toddler's learning, set up regularly scheduled monthly field trips.

What you will need: Transportation, sometimes tickets

How to play: Field trips provide a two-year-old with many new things to think about and discuss. Set aside a certain day each month to take your toddler somewhere interesting. Vary your trips during the year to include:

- ◆ Swimming in a lake, pond, ocean, or public pool
- ◆ Riding on a bus, train, or boat
- ◆ Visiting a farm
- ◆ Shopping at a mall
- ◆ Playing at a friend's house
- ◆ Watching an appropriate movie at a theater
- ◆ Going to a fair
- ◆ Watching a puppet show
- ◆ Attending a children's concert or ballet

Finale

Use the rhyme to sing in the car while traveling to and from field trips. When you need to run errands and your toddler becomes bored in the car, sing rhymes and songs for entertainment. Singing helps pass the time and can be done while you have both hands on the wheel.

Encore

On other occasions, take your toddler to unusual places to eat:

- ◆ Eat at an elementary school cafeteria and watch kids on the playground.
- ◆ Eat at a hospital cafeteria and visit a sick patient.
- ◆ Eat at an airport and watch airplanes take off and land.
- ◆ Buy a hot dog from a street vendor and eat it on the run.
- ◆ Visit a doughnut shop or bakery and have a sweet snack.
- ◆ Take a picnic to the park.

Television Viewing

Everybody's fancy, every body's fine.
Your body's fancy and so is mine.
—Fred Rogers

Overture

Educators believe that children's cartoon shows are often more violent than prime-time adult programs. Studies show that twenty to twenty-five violent acts per hour happen on cartoon-type programs.

Performance

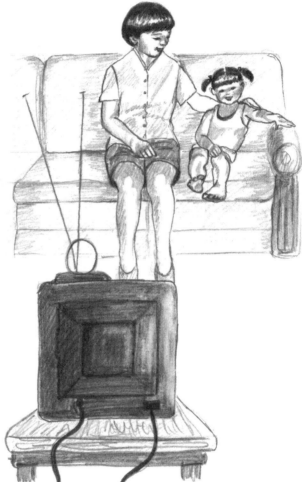

Play: To help your toddler establish good television viewing habits, only allow her to watch educational, non-violent programs.

What you will need: Television

How to play: If your toddler watches television, only allow her to watch programs like reruns of "Mr. Rogers' Neighborhood" or "Sesame Street." Pick programs that are non-violent and educational. Children that are two- to three-years old should not watch more than 15 to 30 minutes of television each day.

Finale

If your toddler is watching television, sit with her and talk about what you are watching. After viewing, help her learn the verses from songs featured on the programs by singing them together. Talk about the program and what she saw.

Encore

Studies have proven that watching violence on television can cause children to act out in aggressive and hurtful ways. In play groups, young children who watch a lot of television are commonly more aggressive and less cooperative than their playmates. You have the power to encourage cooperation, patience, and tolerance in your toddler by never allowing her to view violent programs.

Take Your Pick

Eeny, Meeny, Miney, Moe, catch a monkey by the toe.
If he hollers, make him pay, fifty dollars every day.
—Traditional Rhyme

Overture

Because of their struggles for independence, some two-year-olds have a lot of tension. Giving your toddler many opportunities to make choices will help him gain autonomy and release the feeling of being powerless.

Performance

Play: To help your toddler learn to make choices and celebrate preferences, play "Take Your Pick."
What you will need: Crackers, bite-sized pieces of cheese, fruit slices, raisins, dry cereal pieces, graham crackers
How to play: Place the snack choices on a table. Tell your toddler, "Take your pick." Allow your toddler to make a choice of one or two things. Put the others away. Talk about the toddler's choice, then enjoy the snack. Repeat this process on different days. Each time your toddler "takes his pick," talk about what a good choice it was. "Good for you, you know how to make healthful choices." Describe the flavors of the different foods. You can introduce many new adjectives this way: "crunchy," "sweet," "bitter," "sour," "cold," "hot," "chunky," "smooth," etc. You can help your toddler grow by giving him many opportunities to make decisions. Every afternoon when it is snack time, present the choices and tell him, "Take your pick."

Finale

Filling your toddler's day with opportunities to make choices is important. To help your toddler distinguish between times when he can choose and times when he cannot choose, use verbal cues. "Take your pick" lets him know that he has a choice. If you are giving a command and your toddler cannot choose, you simply say, "This is not a 'take your pick'."
For example:
- When at the bookstore, let your toddler choose a book to buy.
- When at the library, let your toddler choose a book to check out.
- When at a fast-food restaurant, let your toddler choose his drink.
- When at the supermarket, let your toddler help choose some of the foods.

Encore

On a daily basis, give your toddler many opportunities to make choices, especially when asked to do something he does not want to do. For example, taking a bath might not be a choice, but choosing between two or three toys to take into the tub will make your toddler feel like he has some control over the bathing situation. When it is time to get dressed in the morning, let him pick which shirt he wants to wear. The more opportunities he has to make decisions, the more independence he will achieve and transfer into his adult life.

Who's Knocking?

One, two, three, four, someone's at the cottage door;
Five, six, seven, eight, open the door; don't be late.

Overture

Respecting another person's privacy is not something a toddler understands. You will have to teach her the family's rules and set the boundaries that she must respect.

Performance

Play: To teach your toddler to respect a closed door and knock before entering, play "Who's Knocking?"
What you will need: An inside door
How to play: Place your toddler on one side of an inside door. Go to the other side and close the door. Knock or say, "Knock, knock." Then say, "Come in." Open the door. Then repeat the game, letting your toddler invite you to "come in." Take turns knocking and responding to the knock.

Finale

Recite the rhyme while playing the "Who's Knocking?" game. Personalize the words to the rhyme. Example:

One, two, three, four, (toddler's name) at the (family's name) door;
Five, six, seven, eight, open the door; don't be late.

The best way to teach your toddler to respect your rights and privacy is by respecting hers. Begin setting the example of knocking on your toddler's door to get permission to enter the room. Soon she will do the same for you. Respect is a mutual thing that your child can only learn by example.

Encore

The best way to teach your toddler manners is by modeling. Ways a toddler can participate in politeness include:

- Using "please" when asking for something
- Saying "thank you" after receiving something
- Greeting people when they enter a room
- Respecting sibling's possessions by not playing with them unless invited to do so
- Saying "excuse me" when needed
- Apologizing with "I'm sorry" or "sorry" when appropriate

Mealtime Rituals

If all the world was apple pie, and all the sea was ink,
And all the trees were bread and cheese, what should we have to drink?
—Traditional Rhyme

Overture

Instead of three large meals, most toddlers need five small meals a day. Snacks should contribute to your toddler's daily nutritional requirements.

Performance

Play: To celebrate the family and your toddler's enjoyment of family togetherness, establish a meal-time ritual.

What you will need: The family together for mealtimes

How to play: Create special moments to draw the family together. An evening meal ritual of holding hands, singing a song or reciting a poem, or lighting a candle before dinner will help your toddler learn about socialization and experience the feeling of belonging to a family. The rituals you choose to demonstrate will be personal for your family. What ritual you choose is not important; the important thing is to make it a ritual by repeating it when you gather for each family meal.

Finale

Use the rhyme as a pleasant mealtime rhyme or make up one of your own. If family members take turns telling or reading a story at bedtime, this will further strengthen your family unit. Although rituals are time consuming, these special moments will make life more meaningful and will someday be what your child remembers about being part of your family.

Encore

A ritual is considered to be any act done repeatedly over a period of time. Consider adopting one or several of the following as rituals for your family:
- ◆ Throw a kiss good-bye when leaving a room.
- ◆ Invent a silly nonsense word that is used in place of a common word. Example: You might call a jack-o-lantern a "pumpkinman."
- ◆ Create pet names for each family member.
- ◆ Always serve a certain dish on a certain day of the week. Example: Every Wednesday night is pizza night.
- ◆ Each family member has a certain seat around the table.
- ◆ Always pass the food around the table in a certain direction.
- ◆ Everyone shares a wish, dream, or daily event at the evening meal.
- ◆ Serve a favorite dessert on a particular night of the week.
- ◆ Light candles at dinner.
- ◆ Eat lunch on a blanket in the living room one night a month.
- ◆ Ask everyone in the family to help cook one meal each week.
- ◆ Family members might share riddles or jokes at each meal.
- ◆ Everyone kisses the cook after each meal is completed.
- ◆ Each member of the family carries his/her own dishes to the sink after the meal.

Play Groups

There were two blackbirds sitting on a hill.
The one named Jack, and the other named Jill.
Fly away, Jack! Fly away, Jill!
Come again, Jack! Come again, Jill!
—Traditional Rhyme

Overture

Watch your toddler, when you must leave her with a baby-sitter or at a day care center. Does she cry or act out as you are leaving? If she does, do not feel guilty.

Performance

Play: To help your toddler learn social skills from peers, join a play group.

What you will need: A peer group

How to play: A play group enriches a toddler's world and accelerates her learning. When a two-year-old plays with others she can practice being generous, considerate, fair, gentle, and kind. She can begin to learn compassion for other children's feelings and how to share, take turns, cooperate, and solve problems. If there is not a nearby group you can join, consider starting your own play group. If for some reason your toddler cannot be part of a small play group, take her to a park where she can play with peers.

Finale

If your toddler is reluctant to leave your side in the initial play sessions, stay close so she can see that you are nearby. Use the rhyme to encourage her to "fly away," and teach her that you will return. Explain that just like the blackbirds, people go, but then they come back again. Turn the rhyme into a finger play. Use your hands to symbolize the birds.

Example:

There were two blackbirds (*Show fists with thumbs and little fingers extended like the birds' wings.*)

Sitting on a hill. (*Place "birds" on top of knees.*)

The one named Jack, (*Pop right hand up and down, settling back on knees.*)

And the other named Jill. (*Pop left hand up and down, settling back on knees.*)

Fly away, Jack! (*Use right hand like a bird to fly away.*)

Fly away, Jill! (*Use left hand like a bird to fly away.*)

Come again, Jack! (*Bring right hand back to land on knees.*)

Come again, Jill! (*Bring left hand back to land on knees.*)

Encore

Toddlers act on impulse and often cannot make a distinction between appropriate and inappropriate behavior. Your kind words and praises will keep her on the correct path, and your examples will shape her behavior more than any words you speak or rules you set. Remember, affection and love are the most important tools you can use to teach your toddler.

Let's Share

Lucy Locket lost her pocket; Kitty Fisher found it,
Not a penny in it, but a ribbon around it.
—Traditional Rhyme

Overture ....

It is often said that babies can only engage in parallel play. Watch your two-year-old as the year advances, and you will see him begin to interact with others in games of tag, racing, wrestling, ball games, and imaginative play.

Performance ....

Play: To help your toddler learn how to share, play "Let's Share."

What you will need: One toy

How to play: Toddlers enjoy watching other toddlers and older children play, but they are rarely mature enough to engage in cooperative play. A toddler will usually play with his own toy while another toddler plays alongside him with a different toy. During your toddler's third year this will change. Your toddler will begin to interact with peers. Introduce your toddler to the concept of sharing by occasionally playing alongside him with the same toy. When you ask for the toy, say something like, "It is my turn." When you give the toy back, say, "It is your turn."

Finale ....

Use the rhyme to play a cooperation game. Give a soft small purse to the child. Recite the rhyme and then say, "I lost my purse." Then ask, "Did you find it?" On other occasions, practice cooperation and sharing by personalizing the rhyme, and then naming an object that you have handed to your child.
Example:

> Mommy lost her shoe,
> (Toddler's name) found it.
> May I have it back again?

Encore ....

When another toddler comes to play, begin teaching sharing by setting out identical toys or a variety of toys with many parts such as blocks. If your toddler has a favorite "lovie," do not force him to share it with others. It is okay for your toddler to have something that is exclusively his. As adults we have things we will not share with children; people do not have to share everything. The important thing will be teaching your toddler when it is appropriate to share and when it is not necessary. Your example is the best way for your child to understand this difficult-to-learn lesson. When you see your toddler sharing with another person, praise him for his unselfishness.

Punch a Pillow

It's okay to be silly, and it's okay to get mad.
It's okay to be sad; all of my feelings are not bad.

Overture

One way to help your toddler be happy, well-adjusted, and joyful is to let her grow up in a toddler environment rather than an adult environment. If you confront your toddler's behavior with adult standards, she will be unhappy and difficult. If you allow her to be what she is—a baby—you will be giving her permission to do what she does best—be herself.

Performance

Play: To help your toddler understand that she will have negative feelings and help her begin to find ways of dealing with them, play "Punch a Pillow."
What you will need: Pillow
How to play: Toddlers often play out the feelings that are very close to them. When allowed to play out all of their emotions and conflicting feelings without criticism or fear of rejection, they can grow emotionally healthy. In their games, they can take the upsetting feelings they have inside and act them out, to make sense of it all. When your toddler needs to release tension, make a game of punching pillows. She might even benefit from her own punching pillow or crying pillow. Having a "lovie" to use in time of stress will also help your toddler learn to meet her own needs.

Finale

Use the rhyme to remind yourself that children need to learn appropriate ways to deal with their negative feelings. When your toddler acts out her anger in an inappropriate way, calmly explain that it is unacceptable to act out the way she is acting, and then give her a socially acceptable method of expressing her anger. Socially acceptable ways to release tension include:

- Stomping feet
- Singing loudly
- Taking a long walk
- Punching a pillow
- Talking about your feelings
- Dancing wildly
- Running around outside
- Listening to music
- Crying

Encore

Pounding and patting, banging and beating, and squeezing and squashing play clay is a healthy release of energy and tension. Pillow fights and marching to music are also good ways to release physical tension. Show your toddler a variety of appropriate ways to get rid of stress.

Merry Making

Tom, Tom, the piper's son; he learned to play when he was young.
He with his pipe made such a noise, that he pleased all the girls and boys.
—Traditional Rhyme

Overture

Watch your toddler and you will see a little person having a love affair with the universe. Just think, you get to participate in it!

Performance

Play: Use musical instruments to express feelings.
What you will need: Child-sized instruments
How to play: Music is a great way to celebrate life and is an effective outlet for feelings. Through music and dance, youngsters can learn to release tension, celebrate hope, express their uniqueness, and be filled to the brim with joy. You can help the child get a good musical start by:

◆ Providing child-sized instruments
◆ Never suggesting how something "should" sound
◆ Encouraging every potential
◆ Never criticizing his music
◆ Never making unrealistic demands
◆ Not having premature expectations

Finale

Turn the rhyme into a song. Have your child use musical instruments to accompany the verse as you recite it. On other occasions, use musical instruments to sing rhymes and familiar songs, or accompany music played on the radio or CDs. Using musical instruments is an active way for youngsters to enjoy all kinds of music.

Encore

Artistic self-expressions are ways toddlers can express their inner joy. Provide a wide range of mediums for your child to express his happiness in ways he can share with others. Include:

◆ Finger painting
◆ Baking cookies
◆ Making collages of pictures cut from magazines
◆ Jewelry making (stringing beads, pasta shapes, or "o"-shaped cereal pieces)
◆ Printing with paint (fingers, hands, toes, and feet)
◆ Picking flowers and arranging bouquets
◆ Playing in the mud and building, or making pies

170

Paint the Sidewalk

Rosemary green, and lavender blue,
That's the grass and the sky, too.

Overture

Most craft projects are too difficult and take too much skill for two-year-olds, but painting is one artistic endeavor most toddlers can handle and enjoy.

Performance

Play: To help your toddler relax and let go of frustration while celebrating her creativity, paint the sidewalk.

What you will need: Bucket of water, food coloring, one large paintbrush, warm sunny day

How to play: Painting large strokes with a big paintbrush on huge surfaces such as the sidewalk, will help your toddler relax and let go of frustrations. A few drops of food coloring in a bucket of water will make it colorful but will not stain the sidewalk. Show your toddler how to dip the brush in the "paint" and brush it on the sidewalk. Share the brush and talk about sharing while "painting." Change the color of the water a few times during the painting session. Painting does not have to be limited to the sidewalk. Anything with a surface can be painted, such as big rocks, a large plastic playhouse, the bark of a tree, picnic furniture, or a tricycle.

Finale

Use the rhyme to talk about the color of the grass and sky. Find other things that are green and blue. Introduce the primary colors (red, blue, yellow) and secondary colors (purple, green, orange). When describing something, mention its color. Use watercolor paints to express feelings such as "anger," "happiness," "surprise," etc. Talk about feelings and colors. "What color looks angry?" "Which colors make you feel the happiest?"

Encore

On other occasions, be creative in choosing interesting objects as paintbrushes. Encourage your toddler to explore a variety of objects with which to paint, such as:

- ◆ Old toothbrushes
- ◆ Feathers
- ◆ Sponges cut into interesting shapes
- ◆ Soft twigs and branches
- ◆ Leaves

Take Good Care

This is the way I brush my hair, brush my hair, brush my hair.
This is the way I brush my hair and take good care of me.

Overture

There are great individual variations between what a two-year-old and a three-year-old can do for himself. During this third year, your toddler will go from diapers and doing hardly anything for himself to being potty-trained during the day and nearly able to dress himself completely. Demonstrating proper ways to handle each self-care step will make the process easier for your toddler. A little training now will last a lifetime.

Performance

Play: To reinforce self-care skills, play "Take Good Care."

What you will need: Plastic tub, plastic hand mirror, child's hairbrush, comb, soft sponge, hand towel

How to play: Place the items in a plastic tub on the floor between you and your toddler. Pick up the hairbrush and pretend to brush your hair as you recite the rhyme. Then give the brush to your toddler, and recite the rhyme. If he pretends to brush his hair, that is good. If not, help him by placing your hands over his and guide him to brush his hair. Then, demonstrate combing your hair as you recite a revised version of rhyme: "This is the way I comb my hair." Give the comb to your toddler, and have him comb his hair as you recite the rhyme again. Repeat with the soft sponge (wash my face) and hand towel (dry my face).

Finale

Use the rhyme and revised versions of the rhyme to play a guessing game. Recite a verse and have your toddler choose the appropriate tool from the tub and pretend to use it.

Encore

Use the rhyme to encourage the toddler when:
- Brushing teeth
- Taking a bath
- Getting dressed
- Crawling into bed
- Giving hugs/kisses
- Picking up toys
- Eating dinner
- Drinking milk

Baker's Man

Pat-a-cake, pat-a-cake, baker's man!
Make me a cake as fast as you can.
Pat it, and prick it, and mark it with "B,"
And there will be enough for Baby and me.
—Traditional Rhyme

Overture

Since the kitchen is a place that contains many unsafe items, cooking is not an activity that your toddler will often be invited to share. However, while supervised, letting your toddler help make a special dessert for the family will make her feel worthwhile and, at the same time, will be fun for both of you.

Performance

Play: To encourage your toddler to help in the kitchen and feel part of the family, bake sugar cookies.

What you will need: Roll of refrigerated sugar cookie dough, rolling pin, large simple cookie cutter, spatula, can of icing, sprinkles, plastic knife and spoon, baking sheet, floured board

How to play: Begin all kitchen activities by having your toddler wash her hands. How much your toddler helps when baking the cookies will depend on her abilities. Flour a board, and place a small amount of dough on it. Roll out the dough. Show your child how to use a cookie cutter to cut out a cookie. Use the spatula to transfer the cookies to the baking sheet. Repeat until the cookies have all been cut out and placed on the baking sheet. Bake until brown. Carefully remove the baking sheet from the oven and place it where the child will not touch it. When cool, show your toddler how to use a plastic knife to spread a thin layer of icing on each cookie. Top the cookies with sprinkles. Say the rhyme while baking cookies or other desserts in the kitchen. Introduce the letter "B" by drawing it with your finger in the icing on a cookie.

Finale

Use the nursery rhyme to perform a finger play.
Example:
Pat-a-cake, pat-a-cake, baker's man! (*Clap hands.*)
Make me a cake as fast as you can. (*Clap hands.*)
Pat it, and prick it, and mark it with "B." (*Pat, prick, draw a "B."*)
And there will be enough for Baby and me. (*Point to child and self.*)

Encore

On other occasions, use play clay with your toddler. Play clay is a wonderful activity that can keep toddlers busy for hours. A colorful lump, some cookie cutters, and an old rolling pin will inspire your toddler. If you are worried that the toddler will eat the play clay, make Peanut Butter Play Dough. See page 18 for directions.

Boys or Girls?

What are little girls/boys made of?
Sugar and spice and everything nice,
That's what little girls/boys are made of.
　　　　　　　—Traditional Rhyme

Overture

Watch your toddler on one of his "off" days, and you may think you see more spice than sugar. Remember, without the spice how would the gingerbread man taste? Too sweet? Accepting your toddler's basic nature will give him permission to become the person he is meant to be. Children are not cookies to be molded into little adults. Observe your toddler's basic nature and nurture every aspect of his unique personality.

Performance

Play: To reinforce your toddler's gender, play "Boys or Girls?"

What you will need: Magazine with pictures of men, women, boys, and girls

How to play: Sit your toddler on your lap, and hold the magazine where he can see it. Look at the pictures of people and point to a person. Talk about whether the person is a girl or boy. Say something like this: "This is a little girl who will grow up to be a woman" or, "This little boy will someday be a man." Point to pictures and ask: "Woman?" "Man?" "Boy or girl?" Soon the toddler will be able to respond to the pictures of people as male or female.

Finale

Use the nursery rhyme verse to celebrate your child, whether your toddler is a girl or a boy. Personalize the rhyme and recite it as a finger play with your toddler.
Example:
　　What are little girls/boys made of? (*Touch the toddler's cheeks with both hands.*)
　　Sugar and spice, (*Smile and make eye contact.*)
　　And everything nice, (*Kiss the toddler's cheeks.*)
　　That's what little girls/boys are made of. (*Hug your toddler.*)

Encore

On other occasions when out in public, help your toddler distinguish between the women and men, boys and girls, etc. Example: "See that *woman* with the baby?" or "Look at that little *boy* in the sandbox."

This Is Me!

This is me.
Aren't I something!

Overture

As your toddler begins to assert her independence, she will feel some anxiety. She will need to learn to be independent, but at the same time, it will be scary. Celebrating your toddler's abilities will help lessen the insecurities that accompany separation from Mother.

Performance

Play: To encourage your toddler to celebrate her own growth and learning, create a "This Is Me!" photograph album.

What you will need: Camera with film, photograph album

How to play: This project may take several days or a week to photograph, but the final creation will be well worth the time and effort. Dress your toddler in a variety of costumes. As you take photographs, have your toddler demonstrate some of the things she has learned this year including:

- Walking
- Galloping
- Dancing
- Painting
- Drawing with a pencil
- Drinking from a cup
- Putting together a puzzle
- Riding a pedal toy
- Playing with a dolly
- Climbing
- Opening a door
- Putting on shoes
- Hopping
- Standing on tiptoes
- Making music
- Coloring with crayons
- Molding clay
- Eating with a spoon
- Pulling a toy
- Dressing herself
- Rocking a teddy bear
- Walking up stairs
- Bouncing a ball
- Brushing teeth

Finale

When the film is developed, mount one photograph on each page of the album. Use a broad-tipped black marker to write one word or phrase under each photograph. Look at the album and read the words with your toddler as often as she wants to hear it. With great fanfare, bring it out when company comes to your house. Share it with her peers. Cherish it today, and someday she will count it among her greatest treasures.

Encore

Start a collection of your toddler's drawings and scribbling. Begin a scrapbook or glue everything to a large poster board to make a collage. Display her work where family and visitors can see it. Treasuring your toddler's work and praising her accomplishments will build her ego and self-esteem.

Keeping Track

Milestone	Date	Comments
Enjoys outings and field trips		
Favorite television program he/she is allowed to watch		
Shows preferences/ can make choices		
Understands that other people have rights, too		
Enjoys family rituals		
Learns social skills by watching peers		
Understands what it means to share and take turns		
Can release negative feelings in appropriate ways		
Expresses joy in creative ways		
Can relax and play in ways that release tension		
Is learning self-care skills		
Enjoys helping with baking activity		
Knows the difference between boys and girls		
Appreciates and celebrates self-growth and learning		